Say, produce your evidence, if you are true
2(111) Al-Qur'an

THE IRREFUTABLE CHALLENGE OF REALITY

Nature's Evidence about the Ultimate Reality of Allah; And Evidence of Modern Science and Mathematics about the Truth of the Glorious Qur'an and understanding of the Islam as the Universal Natural Religion for Mankind

Atomic Scientist, Engineer
SULTAN BASHIR MAHMOOD
(Sitara-e-Imtiaz)

Copyright © 2009 Sultan Bashir Mahmood

The right of Sultan Bashir Mahmood to be identified as the author of this work has been asserted in accordance with the Copyright, Designs and Patents Act 1988.

All rights reserved. No reproduction, copy or transmission of this publication may be made without written permission. No paragraph of this publication may be reproduced, copied or transmitted save with the written permission or in accordance with the provisions of the Copyright Act 1956 (as amended.) Any person who does any unauthorised act in relation to this publication may be liable to criminal prosecution and civil claims for damage.

Published 2009 by Strand Publishing UK, Ltd.
Golden Cross House, 8 Duncannon Street, Strand, London WC2N 4JF

E-mail address: info@strandpublishing.co.uk
Internet address: www.strandpublishing.co.uk

Paperback ISBN 978-1-907340-04-8

Cover design: Adnan Hanif

Strand Nonfiction

Evidence of nature about the Ultimate Reality of Allah; Perception of Faith in Him; the scientific and mathematical challenges of the Holy Qur'an as a proof of its Revelation from the Creator of the worlds, and understanding of the Islam as a Universal natural religion of mankind for a successful life in this world and the life Hereafter.

PREFACE

We all talk of God. Is He really there? If so what is He like? Where does He live? How does He operate and carry over His orders? How does He control the universe? Why did He make it? Where does man stand in His scheme of creation? Is man a purposeful creation or an accidental product of nature? What is the relationship between God and Man? Did God provide him with His Revelation? What is the proof? Does this Revelation exist even today? What is it?

The spirit behind this work is to look for answers to some of these vital questions on the basis of scientific evidence of reality. It is to help the readers to have an unbiased belief in the fundamental spiritual truths and thus let the inquisitive minds discover *Reality* by themselves in the modern secular environment of today.

It invites the seekers of Truth to look around and listen to the tune of nature as the evidence of their Creator. It also provides irrefutable scientific and mathematical proofs that the Holy Qur'an is indeed that Validated Revelation of the Creator of the worlds, a dire need of the man for the peace of mind and salvation in the Hereafter. But it is not in defence of God, for He does not need one. On the other hand it is to discover our own selves, for our own sake, to know who are we and what best we can do for us?

Sultan Bashir Mahmood (S.I.)
November, 2009
Islamabad.

ACKNOWLEDGEMENTS

This book has been written in memory of my loving mother and caring father, who first taught me to acknowledge, "There is no God but Allah, and Muhammad is the Messenger of Allah"; I confess however, that it took me a long while to discover the true meaning of this statement.

In the compilation of this book, besides my own family, I am very grateful to the following friends for their help. May Allah reward them with guidance to the right path and to the blessings of Jannat (Heaven)in the Hereafter.

1. Brig. (R) Muhammad Hanif, S.I (M), Lahore
2. Col. (R) Bakhtiar Hakeem S. I. (M), Rawalpindi
3. Mr. Muhammad Aslam Khan, Lahore
4. Engr Tariq Masood, Lahore
5. Mr. Shafiullah Khan, Islamabad
6. Arch Jameel Akhtar, Islamabad
7. Farhan Zainulabdin, Lagos
8. Sheikh Shahid Mohsin, Lahore
9. Munir Ahmed Jaunda.

The contribution of Farhan Zainulabdin has been immensely beneficial. He not only reviewed the book but also improved the text in a number of places.

Sultan Bashir Mahmood (S.I.)

TABLE OF CONTENTS

Sr.#	Subject	Pg No
i	Preface	4
ii	Acknowledgement	5
	Part I - The Irrefutable Challenge of Reality	9
01	Mystery and Puzzles	11
02	The First Cause	15
03	Ask the Constants of Nature	19
04	The Challenge of Design	21
05	The Evidence of Water	22
06	The Wonderful Cycle of Water	24
07	What do the Moon and the Oceans Say?	25
08	Listen to the Earth	27
09	The World Around You	29
10	Message from Carbon	30
11	Witness of the Stars in the Heavens, and the Electrons in the Atom	31
12	The Evidence of the Newly Born Baby	32
13	Ask the Honey Bee	32
14	Ask the Little Ants Also	34
15	Marvels of Genetic Mysteries	35
16	Look into Your Own Self	36
17	Ask the Brain	38
18	Evidence of the Vocal Cords, Lips and the Tongue	39
19	What do the Eyes Tell?	40
20	Ask Evolution!	41
21	Believe in Him or Not, He is There	43
22	Towards Understanding Allah *Subhana-Hu*	48
23	Time-Space and Energy Attributes of Allah	49
24	Energy Characteristics of Allah *Subhana-Hu*	53
25	Where Does He Live?	54
26	Can Any Thing Hide from Him?	55
27	Instant Control of Allah *Subhana-Hu*	55
28	Present, Future and the Past are the Same to Him	56

29	What is He Like?	56
30	The Creation of Events	57
	Part II - The Irrefutable Challenge of the Holy Qur'an to Science	59
31	The Glorious Qur'an – A Challenge	60
32	The Qur'an and Science	63
33	Qur'an Provides the Answers	64
34	The Foundation of the Scientific Method	68
35	How Did the Universe Begin?	70
36	Why the Universe and Everything in it?	74
37	The Expansion of the Universe	77
38	A Dynamic Universe	83
39	The Journey of the Sun in the Heavens	87
40	The Universe was a Closed Mass in the Beginning	89
41	Equilibrium and Stability in the Universe	90
42	Primordial Smoky Stuff	93
43	The Universe is Rotating	95
44	The Infiniteness of Creation	99
45	Multi-Worlds and Intelligent Beings	100
46	The End of the Universe	103
47	A Contracting Universe	106
48	The Role of Hidden Matter	108
49	Death is the Final Destiny (Second Law of Thermo Dynamics)	110
50	Space Travel and Space Hazards	113
51	The Absoluteness of Scientific Laws and Programmed Nature	115
52	Quantum Creations	117
53	The Atmospheric Roof	119
54	Protection of the Environment	122
55	Water, The Source of Life	124
56	The Invisible Barrier Between Water Streams	126
57	Existence in Pairs	129
58	Roots of Mountains	131
59	The Qur'an on Human Embryonic Development	133
60	Just Ponder	136

	Part III – The Irrefutable Mathematical	
	Miracles of The Holy Qur'an	139
61	Mathematical Miracles of the Holy Qur'an	140
62	The Relationship between the Solar and the Lunar Years	140
63	The Relationship Between Oceans and the Dry Land on Earth in the Qur'an	142
64	The Miraculous Mathematical Basis of the Holy Qur'an	143
65	The First Revelation and 19	146
66	Miracle of Haroof-e-Muqqatiat – (Special Initials)	147
67	Food For Thought	149
68	Numerical Symmetry of Occurrence of Some Special Words in the Holy Qur'an	151
69	The Miraculous Arrangement of the Holy Qur'an	155
70	Division of the Holy Qur'an into Chapters and Parts	156
71	Significance	160
	Part IV – The Spirit of Islam	163
72	Discovering Islam	164
73	The Universal Natural Religion	166
74	The Essence of Islam	167
75	Peace with Your Creator	171
76	Peace with Yourself	171
77	Peace with Your Neighbour	173
78	Peace with Nature	174
79	To Be At War with Evil	175
80	Spiritual Philosophy of Islam	176
81	A True Muslim – The Vicegerent of Allah Subhana-Hu	179
82	Personality of a True Muslim	180
83	The Man of the Holy Qur'an	183
84	Self Analysis	188
85	A Moment to Pause and Pray	200

Part I

The Irrefutable Challenge of Reality

"Behold! In the creation of the heavens and the earth; in the alterations of the night and day; In the sailing of the ships through the oceans for the profit of mankind; in the rain which Allah sends down from the sky; And the life which He gives there with to an earth that was dead; in living beings of all sorts that He scatters through the earth; in the change of winds and the clouds which trail like their slaves between the sky and earth; there indeed are signs for a people that are wise". (Al-Qur'an Sura 2 – Ayat 164)

01
MYSTERY AND PUZZLES

"Science without religion is lame, Religion without science is blind[1]." (Albert Einstein)

A building reminds you about its architect, a meal about the cook, a book about its author, a painting about the painter. An effect points out to its cause, a machine to its manufacturer and a design to its designer. Yet, there are people who say, "the universe became by itself". Atheists openly say, there is no God. Agnostics say, if He is there, where is He? However, even staunch believers may sometimes wonder, "Is God really there?" "What could He be like?"

Science in its search for "Reality" faces the same dilemma: is the universe an accident, or the product of some objective reality? The order in universe points out to a definite grand design. The chain of causality ends at the big bang, but with the enigmatic query still far from resolution, what was before the big bang? What was the cause of the big bang? Why did it have to be?

The emergence of order out of chaos in the universe is surrounded by mystery. Science says that orderly structures and complex activities that we see today have somehow arisen from the featureless ferment of the big bang. But this is in apparent defiance of the second law of thermodynamics which requires that left at its own, order will turn into disorder with time, unless checked by an

---

[1] Paul Davies, "God and the New Physics" Penguin Books, 1983

external agency. Resolution of this paradox requires the presence of an all-intelligent, ever active super power.

Then there is a host of irritating, so-far unanswered questions, why are the laws of nature as they are? Why does the universe comprise of the things that it does? Like everything within it, will the universe also end? What is beyond physics? What is life? What is mind? Questions such as these, and other similar ones trouble every thinking human being.

The renowned physicist Paul Davies said, *"No scientific pattern is more fundamental or more daunting than those puzzles, how the Universe came into being? Could this have happened without any supernatural input?"* In the answer to this question in the preface of his book, he says, *"It may seem bizarre, but in my opinion science offers a surer path to God than religion"*

The search for ultimate reality doesn't lack enthusiasm. Atheists, secularists and religious people, all speak of some supernatural power, but what is it? Believers call Him Allah, God, Ishwar, Permatma. Agnostics have given Him the names such as "the first cause", "infinity", "the omega point" or "the grand singularity". Atheists appear to be the most confused. To them, He is delusion, the fundamental law of quantum mechanics or simply nothing. All search for Him in their own ways.

Whatever it may be, there comes a point in the search for reality where time and space lose meaning, where the limits of physics snap, and minds boggle. What is beyond that limit of rational human understanding? At this stage an argument starts. Believers say, "It is God". The atheist abruptly jumps in, "I don't believe". The agnostic points out in all earnest, "God might have been necessary in the beginning to create the universe, but not after that He handed it over to the laws of science. There is no role left for Him now. Accept Him or reject, it makes no difference". Then the debate starts over the nature of God, "if He exists, where does He live? What is He made of?" Some even object "if He is a just and loving God, why is there so much misery in the world?"

If it is said, "He is up there", the questioning mind immediately asks, "on what planet...which galaxy?" A Christian priest enters fray, "The loving God, sent His own son to die for our sins". "Could He not forgive the sins without going through that trouble?" asks the Agnostic. The discussion goes on, endlessly. These and many more conundrums concern us deeply in the understanding of our own reality. Indeed our ethics and responsibilities in society depend upon the answers to such fundamental questions.

A lot of the responsibility for this apparent perplexity lies with the priestly classes who assert themselves as mediators between the people and their God. When a Christian priest tells his audience that the creator and controller of the entire universe had a son, born about 2000 years ago to a jewish lady (peace be upon her) in Palestine, whom He allowed to be crucified for our sins, he makes a mockery of the concept of infinite Being of God. And when a Muslim cleric points out, "God is up there", sitting on the throne called "arsh", he limits His omnipotency. Under these circumstances if some people reject such a God in their frustration, they could hardly be exclusively blamed.

Nevertheless, for a thinking human being, evidence in nature for the existence of the Supreme Creator is all pervasive. The complex structures and elaborate organization of the universe, from the whirling galaxies to the heart of the atom, seem to suggest answers to the question, why are things the way they are? why the universe at all, and why the set of laws? Perhaps in asking these questions, we are trying to say that reality is not separate from ourselves. We are a subset of His superset. Just as a subset cannot comprehend the superset, our brains are not made to understand Him.

Science, which deals only with the physical universe, might successfully explain one thing in terms of another but cannot comprehend the Supreme Creator since there is nothing else like Him. Science is predicated on observation. It is fundamentally empirical in characteristic. Without repeatable observation, science becomes speechless. So let us acknowledge quietly, "All praise for Allah, the Designer, Creator and Sustainer of the worlds" الحمدلله رب العالمين. It is only belief that can help us in the quest for Him.

Belief in God is important. Not for Him, but for our own sake, because it makes a huge difference to the meaning of our own lives. If He is there, then He cannot be neglected. If you cannot afford to neglect the boss of your company, how could you get away from the Creator of the universes? If He is there, then He also cannot be unconcerned about you. If you are accountable to the rules of your company, how can you take for granted the Controller of the Universe? If you are accountable to Him, should He not provide you with the criterion to judge upon?

The book in your hands aims to answer some of the questions raised above that eventually leads to exploring the puzzle of our own reality.

Behold, thy Lord said to the angels: "I will create a vicegerent on earth." They said: "Wilt Thou place therein one who will make mischief therein and shed blood? Whilst we do celebrate Thy praises and glorify Thy holy(name)?" He said: "I know what ye know not." [2(30)] Sura Al-Baqra, Ayat 30

02
THE FIRST CAUSE

The universe as understood by science today consists of more than 100 billion galaxies. Each one of these galaxies may in turn contain more than a billion stars. It also appears unlimited in its expanse. Light travelling at the speed of 300,000 km (186,000 miles) / second, cannot reach from one end of this universe to the other, even after billions of years. However, throughout, as science believes today, the universe exhibits a grand order of unity. Wherever man sees, he finds billions of trillions of planets, stars and clusters of galaxies held together in an orderly manner. Who maintains this order?

Everything we come across has a cause for existing. What was the cause of the universe in the first place? Can you say, the universe out of nothing, came into existence by nothing?

Science now claims that some 15 billion years ago, there was no time or space. Then a big bang took place. It was a very precisely determined event. Thereafter the universe began to evolve into an orderly organism and has since then been following certain definite rules, called scientific laws. In following these rules it has thereby grown into countless beautiful worlds of stars and planets.

The famous scientist Paul Dirac said that the "big bang explosion parted off nothingness into matter and anti-matter, *with precisely calculated initial conditions.*"[2]

Who calculated it so precisely?

Who set the laws of science into operation? Who caused the big bang in the nothingness? Science says these questions are out of its domain. Then who will tell us about the Ultimate Reality?

Still no God?

Science believes in the law of cause and effect. It says that everything has a cause in order to come into existence and every event in turn, produces some effect to become another cause. So the chain of causality continues. In the infinite combinations of the causes and the effects at last the search stops at what science calls "Primordial cause", the cause of all causes. Is that the Ultimate Reality?

In their make everything is made up of simpler components. A home is made of bricks, a machine of different materials, and a meal of food ingredients. All of

---

[2] Abd-us-Salam, "Symmetry Concepts of Modern Physics", PAEC Lahore, 1966

them are made of atoms; and atoms in their ultimate of energy; and energy is made of …..???? search stops. So behind every activity there is a simpler more subtle but stronger reality. What is the Ultimate Reality?

Could the universe come into existence out of nothing without it?

Still no God?

After the big bang there was a state of chaos. The universe was a soup of unimaginably hot plasma of matter and energy in transition. It was from this hot transient state that the orderly universe came into existence.

According to the second law of thermodynamics all orderly systems will decay with time into disorderly chaos, unless checked by some external agency, Who then created order in the chaos of the big bang?

Agnostics and atheists say that the universe has evolved by an unending chain of accidents which resulted into eventual creation of order. But according to science, the theory of probability does not support this scenario. Even an infinite number of chances could not produce such prevailing intelligent universal order. *How could the dead produce the living? The darkness the light?*

Still no God?

Science is proud of its discovery of the set of principles of nature, which it calls the laws of science. The genius of modern physics, Dr Albert Einstein, discovered that throughout the time and space continuum, everywhere in the universe, in its past and present, there is only one set of scientific principles. The same physical laws which operate on earth also control the rest of the universe. All scientific predictions, research and analysis are based upon this simple fact. Who in the first place had made the scientific laws and but them in action? Whom do they represent?

Who caused matter and energy to obey them everywhere, all the time, most faithfully?

The oneness of scientific laws is leading science to the concept of grand singularity, a Single Super Unifying Force. Who could be that other than the Primordial First Cause? *If you give it a name what will you call this Ultimate Reality.*

Still no God?

03
ASK THE CONSTANTS OF NATURE

Constants of nature are the most amazing things that science has ever discovered. It has found that the entire universe is functioning as a very sensitively balanced, mathematical orderly system based upon just a few fundamental numbers. If there were even an iota of change in these numbers, the universe as today, could never have come into being, or survived as long as it has.

For example, there are 92 stable elements, each having its own specifically fixed atomic structure, atomic weight and atomic number. Strangely, light or heavy, the number of atoms in every gram atomic weight is always 6.2×10^{24}, called Avogadro number after the name of the scientist who first discovered this fact. As such one gram of hydrogen, sixteen grams of oxygen and 238 grams of uranium, each will always have 6.2×10^{24} atoms.

Who fixed it?

According to Prof Abdus Salam[3] the entire universe is controlled by four forces, the strongest of which is the

---

[3] Abdus Salam "Symmetry Concept in Modern Science", PAEC, Lahore 1966

nuclear force. The next in order of strength is electromagnetic, many times weaker than the nuclear force. The next is the weak force, a million times weaker, and still next the gravitational force, which is a billion, billion, billion times weaker still. All particles can be considered manifestation of these forces.

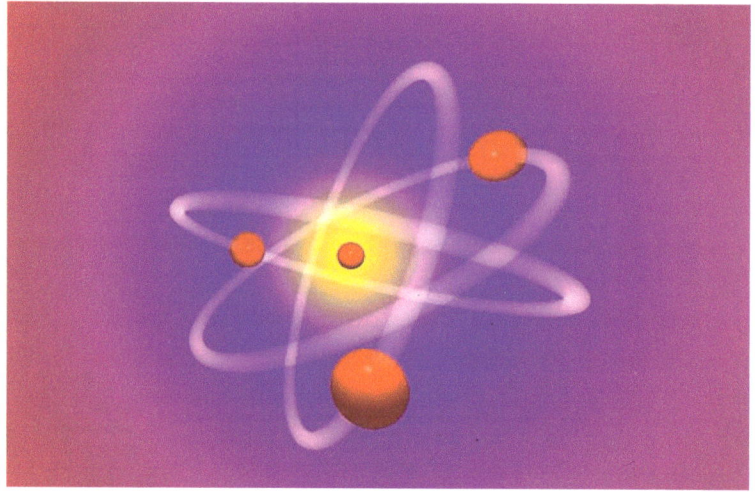

As for their sensitivity, he says, if constants of the gravitational attraction and that of the electromagnetic force had been even slightly different from their given value, even by one in a million, no star could have existed. If the charge on electrons had been even slightly different, atoms would not have formed.

According to Stephen Hawking, "If the density of the universe, one second after the big bang had been greater by one part in a thousand billion, the universe would have re-collapsed after ten years. On the other hand, if the density of the universe at that time had been less by the same amount, the universe would have been essentially empty[4].

Was there any Master Mathematician who before the Big Bang, had precisely calculated designed and then fixed values for constants of nature before the universe had come into existence? And who is holding them unaltered since then?

Is it not strange that atheists say that they agree with scientific laws but not the Lawmaker; acknowledge the absolute control in the universe but not the Controller; witness the marvellous design but do not believe in the Designer!

Still no God?

04
THE CHALLENGE OF DESIGN

Nature on the whole is so designed that the best intellect of the human race put together has not been able to understand it. Wherever science probes, it finds everything working according to a mathematical design which could not be better. Every move is seen as an objective reality. May it be the nucleus of a cell or the unfathomable depths of space; everything is seen following a superbly worked out pre-programmed course. The moon completes its cycle in 29 and ¼ days, the sun goes through the solar spot activity in about eleven years; the earth returns to its original position after one year; radioactive materials radiate with a definite half life. So is human life, following

---

[4] Stephen Hawking "Black Holes and Baby Universe" p 150

its own design. Indeed all of nature, its macro and micro system inclusive, is highly mathematical and chronological.

Could that be possible without of a Super Mathematician?

According to Abdus Salam, *"If we have done anything we hope to have shown that allied with the wonder of God's creation, all explanation we have ever formed is based in symmetry concepts. Whenever faced with two rival theories for the same set of phenomena, one has always found that a theory more aesthetically satisfying is also the correct one. The Holy Qur'an in Sura al-Malik, verses 3-4 has proclaimed the faith of the true scientist,* **'Thou sees not in the creation of the all merciful any imperfection. Return thy gaze; sees thy any fissure? Then return thy gaze again, and again, and thy gaze, comes back to thee dazzled, a weary.'"**[5]

Still doubt God?

05
THE EVIDENCE OF WATER

Everything when freezes shrinks in size and attains higher density. But there is one strange exception. It is the water that you drink. As it cools, it first contracts and gets heavier until it reaches 4°C. Upon further cooling it starts expanding, becomes lighter and solidifies. That is why ice is lighter than the water, and floats like a blanket over it. Thereby, being a bad conductor of heat it does not let the

---

[5] Abdus Salam "Symmetry Concept in Modern Science", PAEC, Lahore 1966

lower layers of water to cool any further. This protects the lakes and oceans from freezing all the way to the bottom.

Imagine the consequences, if water was not exempted from the general rule of continuous shrinking with cooling. Oceans and lakes would have turned into solid blocks of ice. No marine life could have been possible, and ships could not have floated. Moreover, no rains, no fresh water on the ground would have been possible and consequently, no life would have existed on earth. *Who caused this wonderful exception in the natural rules of freezing?*
Is it that water, in sympathy to marine life and the rest of the world, had decided by itself to behave the way that it does?
Still no God?

06
THE WONDERFUL CYCLE OF WATER

Every day the heat of the sun raises millions and millions of tons of sweet water from the salty oceans in the form of vapour. Winds carry it to different lands and pour it down in various forms of precipitation. Thus rain and snow bring sweet water to give life to the dry and barren lands. It helps to keep the atmosphere sufficiently humid, so that we may breathe comfortably.

Moreover, trillions of tons of water are stocked in the form of snow on mountain tops for our use during summer. Sub-soil aquifers are continuously being refilled for man to dig and find water, or through the gushing natural springs. Rivers and streams bring water from the mountains to the alluvial plains and provide fertility to land. Excess water falls back into the ocean. It is a perfect cycle. Everyone's need is being met without wasting a drop. All of this is powered by the "Sun Engine" about one and a half billion kilometres away from us. Without this system life would not have been possible.

Could this be the work of the oceans and the mountains with the approval the Sun?

Still doubt God………………?

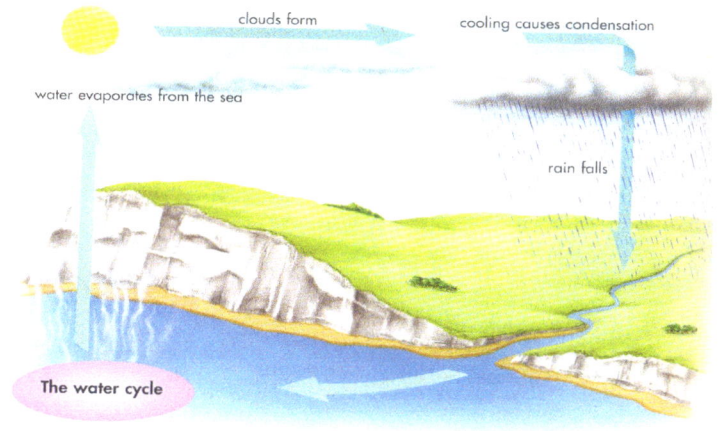

The water cycle

07
WHAT DO THE MOON AND THE OCEANS SAY?

From a distance of 270,000 miles above the earth, the moon performs a daily service of pushing and pulling the waters of oceans, causing ebbs and tides. This is achieved as a result of a complex arrangement of the changing distance of the moon on its orbit around the earth brought about by the axial rotation of earth around itself. Water in the oceans on earth is pulled by the gravity of the moon. This is called tides. When water is pulled up on one side, a depression is created on the opposite side, called ebb. This constant movement of oceans enriches the waters with oxygen and provides sustenance for life within them. It also cleans the harbours, river deltas and seashores by taking the polluted waters to deeper levels. Without this auto-cleaning and washing system oceans would not have been able to support marine life for long. The distance between the earth and the moon is also crucial. Was this lesser, water would have rushed over land, had it been more, tides would have been insufficient.

Did the moon decide this role for itself in sympathy of the oceans on earth for the sake of boosting biological life in them? Or the earth asked moon for this favour?

Still no God?

Seawater is salty to a measured level. This salinity has been maintained within limits over the last three billion years since life began in oceans, to the level necessary for marine life. It makes it easier for them to swim, and also, after dying it disposes of them without smelling foul.

Who established this salt balance in the oceans to effortlessly sustain biological life?

Look into the streams of sweet and saline water flowing side by side in the seas. There are aquifers of sweet and saline water under the surface of earth as well. At places these waters are joined together, yet they do not mix.

Who established this hydro barrier between them to keep them apart?
Just an accident?

08
LISTEN TO THE EARTH

Earth is unique in all respects. It is the only habitable planet on the solar system. This is due to its very position in it that causes a mild climate suitable for life.

The earth revolves around the sun and at the same time also rotates around itself on its axis. In its motion it also spins like a top. If the axes of the earth were at right angles to the path of the earth around the sun, all the days of the year would have been of equal length. This would not have been as good for mankind. In order to create a variety of seasons in a year, the earth is tilted at an angle of 67.5° on its path around the sun. In June, the northern hemisphere is tilted towards the sun and it receives more sunshine during the day. This brings summer, as also winter, spring and autumn during the different periods of the tilt with respect to the sun.

Our survival on earth depends upon this comfortable weather pattern and the regular cycle of day and night. Imagine, if it were not like that, could life have been possible?

Who determined and tilted the earth at precisely 67½ degrees at its orbit around sun? Who fixed an elliptical orbit for it instead of a circular one in order to produce variations in seasons on it? Who maintain it so precisely?

Who made it rotate on its own axis once in 24 hours to produce the cycle of day and night?

Did the earth decide all this for itself?

Still no God?

The inner core of earth is made of molten iron which is the cause of the massive electric currents in it This in turn is responsible for lightning in the clouds that converts free nitrogen into nitrous oxide, necessary for the growth of food and flora. Moreover, this feature also allowed the invention of magnetic compass, which in turn contributed to the invention of submarines, aircrafts among others by helping to orient and track their paths and destinations. What a design! Who did it?

The same magnetism causes a very strong protective cover of ionosphere over earth, which shields life on it from the harmful radiation of outer space. Moreover, it reflects radio waves back to earth allowing long distant radio communication possible. Imagine if earth was not like that! Did this happen by chance?
Still doubt God?

09
THE WORLD AROUND YOU!

The earth's original atmosphere contained poisonous gases. The lack of oxygen meant that animals or plants could not have survived. Along came the algae, a plant-like bacteria, which released oxygen through the process of photosynthesis. Thus, gradually, the atmosphere was made fit for life to appear on earth.

Each plant that grows on earth is directly beneficial for us. These are factories made to receive solar energy, and convert it into food for us to eat, and grow the wood for us to burn. They suck carbon dioxide from the air, then retain one atom of carbon and in return give out two atoms of oxygen back to the environment.

Who programmed all this? The oceans, the algae? If you your answer is 'evolution', then who guided evolution to evolve things in the way that was necessary?

Still no God?

10
MESSAGE FROM CARBON

Our body is primarily made of carbon. How did this basic building block of life come into existence? Science has now discovered that carbon atoms in your bodies were formed in some remote star by a very special process. When three atoms of helium are fused together at ultra high temperature and pressure, one atom of carbon is formed. It is further discovered that fusion reaction is made possible by precisely determined resonance of helium atoms at a special frequency. Had there been even a minute mismatch in the mutual resonance of these elements, they would not have joined together to make carbon. Consequently, no energy, no carbon, no plants, no animals, no humans would have existed.

Who masterminded this grand design of creation? Who fixed for helium this special frequency of resonance to make the fusion of elements possible? Who maintains these ultra precise conditions even fifteen billion years later?

Did helium think of that itself, or did carbon ask for it?

Still no God?

11
WITNESS OF THE STARS IN THE HEAVENS, AND ELECTRONS IN THE ATOM

Modern science has discovered that everything in nature is in motion. Electrons within the atom dart around the nucleus. Planets go round stars, and constellations are moving in the galaxies. Everything is floating in space on pre-destined and pre-programmed courses.

Our sun also along with its ten planets, twenty-seven moons, and millions of meteorites, keeps moving on its course in space at a fantastic six hundred miles per second. In this breakneck journey, no one oversteps the rights of others.

Rotation is necessary for the survival of all these bodies. If anyone stops, it will be devoured by the gravity of its nearest companion and destroyed. It provides the repulsive, centrifugal force emanating from the centre of each body in motion, in order to balance the forces of gravitation and electron charge. Hence all heavenly bodies are kept in their position caught by the counteracting forces.

Who designed this enduring, finely balanced system and *who maintains such fine and precise order in the Universe?*

Did the planets and the stars programme for themselves?

Still you deny the Ultimate Reality of God?

12
THE EVIDENCE OF THE NEWLY BORN BABY

The behaviour of new born life is fascinating. Who teaches the baby to cry to draw the attention of its mother other than God? Who gives fortitude to the mother to face every challenge to the life of its offspring so bravely other than God? A mother sparrow can stand eye-ball to eye-ball with an eagle in order to protect her chicks. *Who gives her this courage? Who teaches the chicks to start walking soon after hatching? Who prepares the cow to feed the calf before its birth?*

Who makes the offsprings of mammals dart to their mothers' mammary glands immediately after birth? There is no teaching, no training, but they know exactly what to do! Who teaches them other than God?

Still no God?

13
ASK THE HONEY BEE

If still in doubt about God, then ask the little honey bee who made her and who taught her to make honey that is perfectly and deliciously edible for us?

This little creature is a miracle of design and a wonder of performance. She searches for nectar far and wide, travelling miles, sucking flower to flower, each time collecting a few micrograms in her belly. In return, the honey bee helps flowers to produce fruit by pollinating their male and female genes.

She is aware of the science of poisons and thus never touches a poisonous flower. She is a master chemist who knows the art of separating honey for food and wax for building its hive.

She is an expert air conditioning engineer as well, quite aware of the science of heating and ventilation. During hot weather, she knows how to keep the honey cool in order to prevent it from flowing out of the hexagonal cubicle stores and during the cold winter, she works as a thermostat to stop the honey from freezing.

She is also a superb civil engineer. Her hexagonal houses are magnificent pieces of art and architecture. She is also a master par excellence of sociology and management. Thousands of honey bees work in tandem under the leadership of one queen – nobody has ever heard of strikes, quarrels or any other form of mismanagement amongst them so far!

The honey bee's skills of remote sensing and mutual communication are mind boggling. She is equipped with a marvellous system of distance tracking and direction keeping, so she flies back to her home without losing way. Her defence system is no less astounding. The way they perform guard duties around their home will amaze any highly trained security expert. Within the spirit of caring and sharing, the mutual team work between honey bees truly is astonishing.

Who taught the little bee other than God, the wondrous technology of making honey? Brainless evolution or some Mastermind?

If you are still not clear, then try asking the spiders. They are excellent weavers. Who has taught them to weave matchless fine web? The only tool they have for this unparalleled product is their specialized salivary glands!

Still no God?

14
ASK THE LITTLE ANTS ALSO

This tiny creature is a miracle of creation, clever and efficient and has far outlasted the dinosaurs. In her skills she is a marvel of science and technology. Ants live in a highly organized way, like soldiers in an army cantonment.

Who has taught them other than God the norms of mutual caring and sharing and the canons of living together as a civilized community? Who educated them other than God in the safety rules and environmental laws, and who taught them weather forecasting so that they rush to safety before it rains? Ask them also who had assigned them the job of clearing refuse and waste foods from the floor? Imagine a world without their services!

Still no God?

15
THE MARVELS OF GENETIC MYSTERIES

In an adult human being about three trillion cells work together in perfect harmony for a healthy life. Each cell knows exactly what to do, and where to fit in. It is a wondrous computer with its own power source. Moreover, a human body is an incredible factory producing millions of new cells daily to replace the worn out ones so that the system stays fresh.

A baby's genetic makeup is decided right from the time when the egg is fertilized by the male sperm. The crucial activity of cell division involves the nucleus. Each nucleus contains two sets of genes: one comes from the father and one from the mother. Before a cell divides, both sets of genes are copied in a process termed as DNA replication. Thus new cells receive a full double set of genes, one from the father and one from the mother. The life of the organism then unravels according to the programme stored in its genes.

Could this precise pre-programmed development of living organisms be the work of evolution when by its own admission the theory of evolution works only in the long run counted in terms of millennia and when life would have no chance of survival without transferring of genetic traits even from one generation to the next?

Not only that, every cell is like a seed, a complete personality in itself. It is made to grow, multiply and integrate with billions of other cells to become a complete human child in the watery sack of its mother's womb. What an automatic wonderful factory to produce human beings! Although there are billions of humans, yet each is unique within itself.

A microscopic cell turns into a full sized, muscular, talking, walking genius.

Who is behind all this?

We plan all our tasks, but when it comes to the complex development our own selves, some say, it happened accidentally. Could there be a more bogus claim than that?

16
LOOK INTO YOUR OWN SELF

Our body is a wonderfully packed bio-factory in which millions of life giving chemical reactions constantly takes place. Our pancreas does not let the level of sugar in our blood go beyond certain limits. The heart pumps blood to each cell of the body untiringly for the entire length of its life. It beats around forty million times a year, about three billion times in an average life span, without needing repair.

Who made such a rugged pumping system?

Think also of the kidneys. They know what to filter out and what to retain in the blood. So are the stomach and the liver, miraculously designed factories which convert food into blood, proteins and hydrocarbons needed for our nourishment.

Then consider the lips, tongue, eyes, ears and nose. How hundreds of movements of muscles are coordinated to perform their functions?

Who is that master designer and expert manufacturer that put them together to work in such breathtaking complex harmony?

Imagine the miraculous control of the wind and food pipes in the throat. How one closes when the other opens to direct food to the stomach and air to the lungs. Which of the favours of your Creator will you then deny?

Think of the delightful taste buds in our mouth. Thousands of them are scattered along the tip, sides, and back of the tongue. We have around 10,000 taste buds on our tongue only. Each one is microscopic bunch of about 50 cells which have furry, frilly tips and are divided into four main groups to detect sweet, sour, salty and bitter tastes located on different areas of the tongue. When molecules land on the frilly tip, the taste bud cells send out elective signals. These signals pass along small nerves which gather into two main nerves and then travel along these to the taste-conscious area in the brain.

Could this be the work of the blind evolution?

Now look at the spleen which is one of the main filter systems for the blood. Not only it filters out the dead cells, but removes the abnormal ones also. This applies in particular to the red blood cells, but white cells and platelets are also filtered selectively by the spleen when it is necessary. The spleen also plays a major role in the manufacture of new red blood cells for people with bone marrow disease. It also manufactures a large part of the blood for the foetus while it is in the uterus during its gestation period.

Look also into the mystery immune system of your body. In spite of all scientific knowledge, it is still not understood even by expert doctors.

Who could so thoroughly design, construct and integrate to gather your body for its wondrous functions other than God? What makes you doubt in Him?

17
ASK THE BRAIN

Bubbly, greyish dough, locked safely in a spherical box of bones, it floats in a delicately balanced fluid of minerals. It is an absolutely unrivalled intelligent supercomputer which gathers, stores, analyzes, processes and takes decisions. It remains active at work 24 hours of the day and 365 days of the year. All our inventions, scientific discoveries, creative works, poetry, philosophy and of course our super computers, internet, space crafts and all other scientific developments are the brainchild of this wisdom pack in the human head.

Even then some say, "Man in another animal". "It is as accidental product of evaluation". What an insult to human intellect!

If an ordinary computer needs hundreds of highly trained people to design and make it, how could it be, that the wondrous computer called the human brain, became by itself, needed no designer, no creator?

How come mindless evolution made this wisdom pack for us? If you are a die hard evolutionists then think why did it work for the man only, and other animals were conviently left for behind?

Will you still not believe in God?

18
EVIDENCE OF THE VOCAL CORDS, LIPS AND THE TONGUE

As air flows out of the lungs, we use it to make unlimited sounds, words and rhythms. At the top of the windpipe, at the sides of the voice box or larynx, are two stiff shelf-like folds – called vocal cords. Criss-crossed muscles in the voice box can pull them together so that air passes through a narrow slit between them and make them vibrate. As the vocal cords are pulled tighter, they make higher-pitched sounds. As they loosen, they produce lower-pitched sounds. Our speech function depends on the signal to and from the brain and its ability to differentiate in the sounds that we emanate.

Even a minor invention needs a genius to make it. Who is the inventor of this unique system of intelligent talking? Could it be some one other than an All-wise God? Still doubt Him?

19
WHAT DO THE EYES TELL?

They are the body's window to the world. Like a video camera they detect the moving world around us and turn this picture into tiny electrical signals. These signals are nerve impulses which go to the brain to be sorted. Every second or two, eyelids blink and sweep tear fluid across the conjunctiva, washing away dust and germs.

The image that forms on the retina when light passes through the lens is upside down, because of the way in which light rays are bent by the eye's lens. The brain automatically turns the image the right way up, but we are never aware that this is happening.

It making of a video camera has been the result of the efforts of great number of highly capable scientists and engineer, how come the wonderful camera of the eye became by itself?

How unfortunate, that still some people insist that man is a genetic accident. No design, no planning, just by a slow trial and error process of chemical combinations and environmental reactions, over a long period of time he became a walking genius by evolution. Will you believe it?

Still doubt God?

20
ASK EVOLUTION!

Did you create the protective layer of ozone gas, seven hundred miles above us to save us from the damaging ultraviolet rays of the sun? Life on earth would roast without this protective umbrella.

Is the critical distance between the sun and earth, also the brainchild of evolution to ensure perfect temperature and to maintain the required energy balance for the nourishment of life on earth?

Did evolution also create the buffer of atmosphere around the earth that extends up for thousands of miles and that helps burn hazardous shooting meteors before they hit the surface of earth?

Did evolution also teach the plants to use solar light for photosynthesis of carbon dioxide and water to produce food and generate oxygen for biological life to survive on earth?

If survival is for the fittest, why are there millions of competing species of plants and animals, living and developing together since billions of years on earth? Who keeps the population balance between them? Who had produced the primal single cell to begin with? Who directs evolution?

What about the earthly resources, its minerals, atmosphere, environment, fauna and flora necessary to support each other? Did evolution make them?

Who creates every one of us, unique? Who produces the wonderful symmetry in the assembly of billions of human beings? No two finger prints match one another, yet they have many similarities and commonalities. Is it the work of evolution also?

Such is the creation of Allah. If still not sure then ask Mr. Doubtful!

According to the second law of thermodynamics, of science "entropy or disorder in any system must increase with time, unless and until it is compensated by some appropriate external agency". If this is true then how could disorder create order from the chaos of big bang, without some external supernatural power?

How could darkness bring light?
How could nothingness cause something?
How could dead give birth to the living?
How could brainless atoms of matter produce an intelligent being like you?

Will you still not believe in God?

Creation, the like of man is not an isolated event. It required integration of millions of causes. For example, our bodies are produced from the dust created in a series of stellar explosions; it needed a sun, a very typical middle level star, placed at a very special position in our galaxy; it also required an earth-like planet which is unique in many respects; this in turn needed the very specially configured moon, so on, so forth. Thus life produced on earth is not an isolated event but the result of innumerable, very sensitive, closely interrelated, integrated events and parameters Specialists in the theory of probability say that such a complex, sensitively balanced and integrated system of uncountable causes and effects is simply impossible.

Who is the one who had created and then integrated all these millions of necessary events and then guided the nature to achieve the outcome in front of us? Who is the mastermind behind this entire highly complex systems engineering?

Blind evolution? Is it the name of your God?

21
BELIEVE IN HIM OR NOT, HE IS THERE

Indeed everything in the universe is compelling evidence about its all wise, all knowing designer, integrator, systems engineer, maker, nourisher, controller, sustainer and supreme operator. He is Allah, the God of everything. About Him the Holy Qur'an says,

> *"Of Him seeks (its needs) whatever is there in the Universe. Each day He shines in new Splendour" 55(29).*

Indeed, may it be a petal or a sepal, or a drop of water, all extol the glory of their Creator. Laws of science are His orders, the universe is His domain. Future, present and past are one to Him. All measures are His. When He wants to do something, He simply says, "Be" and it is there. Kind and Merciful always to believers and non believers, agnostics and atheists alike; – as He says in the Holy Qur'an *"Indeed We have honoured Mankind"*.

HE IS ALLAH!

He looks after them without their asking. Ever-living, All-encompassing, Grand Singularity. The Supreme Integrator, the Grand System Engineer, Supreme Creator and Sustainer of everything. The Total Control, the Omnipresent, the Omniscient, All-knowing, All-wise, All-Powerful, Ever Active, He is The Ultimate Reality.

HE IS ALLAH!

The One and the only, without any partner, free of all faults, and supreme in all qualities. The First Cause; has no father, no mother, no son or daughter. The Absolute Singularity, Infinite Whole. There is nothing like unto Him. Through there is no example to describe Him, but everything in nature is evidence of His Supreme Reality. He also sent His human messengers to mankind to remind them of Him and to testify His Existence everywhere. These were the most truthful people. The last of them was Muhammad (peace be upon him), who taught mankind. *"Your God is One. The Most Kind, and the Most Compassionate. Sustains all, even those who deny Him. If you oblige His creatures He says, 'You have obliged Me.' If you spend in His way, He says, 'You have given to Me.' His patience is boundless even for those who defy Him; The best friend, closer than your jugular vein."*

HE IS ALLAH!

There are not enough words to describe Him, no eyes to see Him, no vision to comprehend Him. Nevertheless, you can feel the grandeur of His presence everywhere. He is Allah!

How sad! We live in His sovereignty, but violate His rules!
He surrounds us all around, but we do not realize it!
We come from Him and go back to Him, but are not afraid of Him!
We seek the knowledge of things, but forget the Creator!
We look for the purpose behind everything, but hardly care to know about our own purpose of existence.
We believe in the laws of conservation of mater, energy and momentum but doubt life Hereafter?

Don't forget Mr. Doubtful! God exists, He is everywhere. Every atom of matter, every photon of energy hymn His Glory. We are His wonderful creation, not a meaningless entity. Each one of us is His idea, and life is His gift to us. One day we will have to answer the big question, what did we do with it?

Let us be reminded again.

اِنَّ اللّٰهَ فَالِقُ الْحَبِّ وَالنَّوٰى ۚ يُخْرِجُ الْحَىَّ مِنَ الْمَيِّتِ وَمُخْرِجُ الْمَيِّتِ مِنَ الْحَىِّ ۚ ذٰلِكُمُ اللّٰهُ فَاَنّٰى تُؤْفَكُوْنَ ۞ فَالِقُ الْاِصْبَاحِ ۚ وَجَعَلَ الَّيْلَ سَكَنًا وَّالشَّمْسَ وَالْقَمَرَ حُسْبَانًا ۚ ذٰلِكَ تَقْدِيْرُ الْعَزِيْزِ الْعَلِيْمِ ۞ وَهُوَ الَّذِىْ جَعَلَ لَكُمُ النُّجُوْمَ لِتَهْتَدُوْا بِهَا فِىْ ظُلُمٰتِ الْبَرِّ وَالْبَحْرِ ۚ قَدْ فَصَّلْنَا الْاٰيٰتِ لِقَوْمٍ يَّعْلَمُوْنَ ۞ وَهُوَ الَّذِىْ اَنْشَاَكُمْ مِنْ نَّفْسٍ وَّاحِدَةٍ فَمُسْتَقَرٌّ وَّمُسْتَوْدَعٌ ۚ قَدْ فَصَّلْنَا الْاٰيٰتِ لِقَوْمٍ يَّفْقَهُوْنَ ۞ وَهُوَ الَّذِىْٓ اَنْزَلَ مِنَ السَّمَآءِ مَآءً ۚ فَاَخْرَجْنَا بِهٖ نَبَاتَ كُلِّ شَىْءٍ فَاَخْرَجْنَا مِنْهُ خَضِرًا نُّخْرِجُ مِنْهُ حَبًّا مُّتَرَاكِبًا ۚ وَمِنَ النَّخْلِ مِنْ طَلْعِهَا قِنْوَانٌ دَانِيَةٌ وَّجَنّٰتٍ مِّنْ اَعْنَابٍ وَّالزَّيْتُوْنَ وَالرُّمَّانَ مُشْتَبِهًا وَّغَيْرَ مُتَشَابِهٍ ۚ اُنْظُرُوْٓا اِلٰى ثَمَرِهٖٓ اِذَآ اَثْمَرَ وَيَنْعِهٖ ۚ اِنَّ فِىْ ذٰلِكُمْ لَاٰيٰتٍ لِّقَوْمٍ يُّؤْمِنُوْنَ ۞ وَجَعَلُوْا لِلّٰهِ شُرَكَآءَ الْجِنَّ وَخَلَقَهُمْ وَخَرَقُوْا لَهٗ بَنِيْنَ وَبَنٰتٍ بِغَيْرِ عِلْمٍ ۚ سُبْحٰنَهٗ وَتَعٰلٰى عَمَّا يَصِفُوْنَ ۞ بَدِيْعُ السَّمٰوٰتِ وَالْاَرْضِ ۚ اَنّٰى يَكُوْنُ لَهٗ وَلَدٌ وَّلَمْ تَكُنْ لَّهٗ صَاحِبَةٌ ۚ وَخَلَقَ كُلَّ شَىْءٍ ۚ وَهُوَ بِكُلِّ شَىْءٍ عَلِيْمٌ ۞ ذٰلِكُمُ اللّٰهُ رَبُّكُمْ ۚ لَآ اِلٰهَ اِلَّا هُوَ ۚ خَالِقُ كُلِّ شَىْءٍ فَاعْبُدُوْهُ ۚ وَهُوَ عَلٰى كُلِّ شَىْءٍ وَكِيْلٌ ۞

It is Allah Who causes the seed-grain and the date-stone to split and sprout. He causes the living to issue from the dead, and He is the One to cause the dead to issue from the living. That is Allah: Then how are ye deluded away from the Truth?

He it is that cleaves the daybreak (from the darkness of night):

He made the night for rest and tranquillity, and the sun and moon for the reckoning (of time): Such is the judgement and ordering of (Him), the Exalted in Power, The Omniscient.

It is He Who maketh the stars (as beacons) for you, that ye may guide yourselves, with their help, through the dark spaces of land and sea: We detail Our Signs for people who know.

It is He Who hath Produced you from a single person: Here is place of sojourn and a place of departure: We detail Our Signs for people who understand.

It is He Who sendeth down rain from the skies. With it We produce vegetation of all kinds: From some We produce Green (crops), out of which We produce grain, heaped up (at harvest); out of the date-palm and its sheaths (or spathes) (come) clusters of dates hanging low and near:

And (then there are) gardens or grapes, and olives, and pomegranates, each similar (in kind) yet different (in variety): When they begin to bear fruit, feast your eye with the fruit, and the ripeness thereof. Behold! In these things there are Signs for people who believe.

Yet they make the Jinns equal with Allah, though Allah did create the Jinns; and they falsely, having no knowledge, attribute to Him sons and daughters. Praise and glory be to

Him! (For He is) for beyond that they attribute to Him!

To Him is due the primal origin of the heavens and the earth: how can He have a son when He hath no consort? He created all things, and He hath full knowledge of all things.

That is Allah our Lord! There is no god but He, the Creator of all things: Then worship ye Him only: and He has power to dispose of all affairs.
(Sura Al-Inaam, Ayaat 95-102)

22
TOWARDS UNDERSTANDING ALLAH *SUBHANA-HU*

From the ubiquitous evidence of nature, no sane person can deny the reality of Allah. Everything in the universe is witness to His Supreme Being. But what is He? Where is He? Is He also made of matter and energy like us?

Some of the illustrious prophets (peace be upon them all) in the past had also asked similar questions. For example, Ibraheem (Abraham PBUH) is mentioned in the Holy Qur'an as requesting Allah to show how He brings the dead to life. The illustrious prophet Musa (Moses PBUH) also asked to show him His own self.

Since man's knowledge is restricted, so it will never be possible for us to comprehend His absolute reality fully. As the Holy Qur'an says, He is absolutely unique in all respects, **"There is nothing like unto Him" 112(5).** He is the superset and we are just a tiny subset of His domain. So the Holy Qur'an says, *"Vision Comprehends Him not, but He comprehends (all) vision. He is Subtle, all Knowing" 6(104).* Thus the only way we may know our Creator is through His creation. It is similar to how we develop an instinctive sense of the painter from his paintings and of the author from his writings.

On this subject the guidance revealed in the Holy Qur'an is very clear. In hundreds of ayaat (statements of the Qur'an, *lit* a sign, *pl*), man is advised to reflect into the universe, to appreciate its Creator. An example is ayat 164 of sura al-Baqara,

> *Lo! In the creation of the heaven and the earth and in the succession of night and day, and in the ships that speed through the seas with what is of use to man, and in the water which Allah sends down from the sky, thereby giving life to the earth that had been lifeless and causing all kinds of living creation upon it, and in the change of the winds, and in the clouds between the sky and the earth – all these are signs (of Allah) for people who use their reason [2(164)]*

Allah *Subhana-Hu* introduces Himself in the Holy Qur'an with over one hundred of His qualitative attributes. We can understand the working of our Creator through these attributes though cannot know Him in person.

23
TIME-SPACE AND ENERGY ATTRIBUTES OF ALLAH

The most perceptible-by-attribute understanding of Allah *Subhana-Hu* given in the Holy Qur'an is by the time, space and energy characteristics. In this respect Muhammad (PBUH) made a very enlightening remark. He is reported to have said, "Do not curse time, for Allah Himself is time" (*Hadith*). In this context, ayat 3 of sura al-Hadid is most thought provoking,

هُوَ الْأَوَّلُ وَالْآخِرُ وَالظَّاهِرُ وَالْبَاطِنُ وَهُوَ بِكُلِّ شَىْءٍ عَلِيْمٌ

He is 'The Very First' and 'The Very Last'; And (He is) 'The Outermost' and 'The Innermost'; And He is knower of each and everything [57(3)]

In this ayat, the phrases, 'The Very First' (الأوّل) and 'The Very Last' (الآخر) relate to the time dimension. The One who at the same moment is, "The First" and "The Last", cannot be but the absolute time itself. Similarly, the attributes 'The Outermost' (الظاهر) and 'The Innermost' (الباطن) relate to the space dimension. The personality which exhibits these two attributes simultaneously can only be the One that encompasses the total space. This deduction is also supported by the often repeated ayat of the Holy Qur'an ان الله على كل شئ محيط *"Indeed Allah encompasses each and everything"*.

The phrase كل شئ (each and everything) leaves no exception. Allah is inside and simultaneously outside everything. From subatomic particles to the entire universe, everything forms a subset to His great Reality.

> *So we may say that time and space are two attributes of Allah Subhana-Hu through which He manifests His grand reality in the physical world. To Him belongs the absolute Time and the absolute Space.*

There is also the law of pairs as given in the Holy Qur'an which says that Allah *Subhana-Hu* creates things on the pattern of pairs (sura Yasin, ayat 36),

> **Limitless in His Glory, He who has created pairs in whatever the earth produces, and in your own kind, and in that of which (as yet) they have no knowledge [36(36)]**

In this ayat use of the phrase كل شىئ means that there is no exception to this rule. We may say that Big Bang was the revelation of the Singularity of Allah *Subhana-Hu* through the pair of His time-space attributes. That was the initial manifestation of intersection between the metaphysical and the physical worlds. For example, as per general theory of relativity, gravity is pimply a property of space, not a force. Infact universe on the whole is the property of space-time dynamism. From here the pair of mass and energy was created that is interrelated according to the relationship $E=Mc^2$, discovered by Einstein in 1904. All this happened suddenly when Allah ordered the universe, 'Be' and it came into being (كن فيكون). The figure below is an attempt to represent this great beginning:

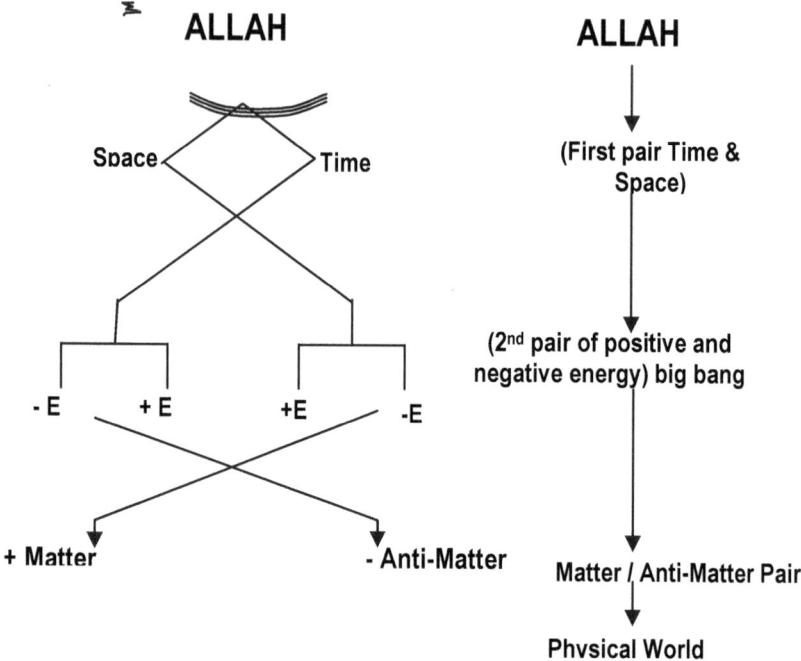

This explains the pre-big bang universe and the space-time riddle. We may say that before the universe came into physical existence, there was a software phase of existence when everything was designed by Allah *Subhana-Hu*. Time and space were also hidden in the personality of the Supreme Creator. With His command, "Be", He manifested Himself from the pre-universe state of metaphysical order into the post-big bang physical world. In one of his saying, Muhammad (PBUH) distinguished the spiritual dimension about creation that in the pre-universe stage, Allah *Subhana-Hu* was alone like a hidden treasure; He willed that He should be known, so He decided to create Man and Universe for him. Thus the design basis of the Universe is Man. He is the very reason therefore He created it, not the product of it.

24
ENERGY CHARACTERISTICS OF ALLAH *SUBHANA-HU*

Besides time and space, the third fundamental characteristic of Allah *Subhana-Hu* is His energy attribute, called Noor (نور) in the Holy Qur'an. In sura an-Noor, ayat 35, the Holy Qur'an refers to Him as 'Noor upon Noor' نور على نور.

In metaphysical terms Noor means 'spiritual light'. In the physical world it means light energy. In the physical sense Muhammad (PBUH) is reported to have said that Allah is veiled by seventy layers of His Noor. If only one of them is removed, His Noor will vaporize the entire world. The Holy Qur'an tells us about the prophet Musa (PBUH), when upon His insistence, Allah *Subhana-Hu* projected some of His glory at a mountain, it exploded. This suggests that Allah *Subhana-Hu* is the infinite source of spiritual as well as the physical energy.

Thus the fundamental characteristics by which we may comprehend His Supreme Reality are the time, space and energy attributes. Every event in the physical world is a manifestation of a combination of these three ingredients – they are the essential inputs for any event in the universe to occur.

From here we may say that Time-Space continuum is a very dynamic pair, whose interaction releases energy. Thus production of energy is a function of interaction between time and space, viz $e = f(ts)$, being released since Big-Bang and continually added in the universe, manifesting itself through matter and anti-matter, as per the legendary equation discovered by Einstein, $e = mc^2$. This explains the reason behind the continuous expansion of the universe and eventual reason for its contraction and collapse.

25
WHERE DOES HE LIVE?

Many would say that Allah lives up in the skies. They indicate Him usually by pointing their index figure upward, as if Allah *Subhana-Hu* resides in some planet in the heavens. You might also have seen paintings in Christian Churches showing God floating in heaven, sporting a big beard. But He is not like that at all. It is inappropriate to draw His pictures or limit Him to a specific place. If He occupies a place then He is contained by that place which is contrary to His basic attribute of being Omnipresent. However, to be conscious of the fact that total space itself is one of the attribute of His personality makes it easy to understand that He pervades everything. May it be the fundamental particles of the atom or the entire universe, He is everywhere; Omnipresent, Omniscient. He is the Outermost, and the Innermost and so He encompasses everything from all sides. Since He is infinite, so every point in space can claim the honour of being His centre.

26
CAN ANY THING HIDE FROM HIM?

From His time-space attributes we can also see that everything exists in Him. Nothing can be outside of Him. You may imagine this by the example of a fish in the ocean: water is in and water is outside of it. Can thus fish ever hide from the water? Similarly, Allah *Subhana-Hu* encompasses everything from inside and outside. Therefore, spatial states of 'here and there', 'up and down', 'far and near' are meaningless in the context of His presence.

He does not need to travel to reach anywhere, and neither does He need to ask someone else for any information. Nothing at all, not even a single atomic particle can hide from Him. He surrounds each and every particle of matter and photons of energy – all the time, everywhere, from inside as well as outside.

27
INSTANT CONTROL OF ALLAH *SUBHANA-HU*?

You know that Time and space are the two essential ingredients for any physical event to take place. Space provides the accommodation and time provides the duration for the event to occur in the universe. Without these inputs nothing can take place. Thus time gives life to the event and space provides housing for its manifestation. As time and space are a subset of the Grand Reality of Allah *Subhana-Hu*, therefore, nothing can happen without Him. Neither a drop of rain water, nor a leaf from a tree can fall without His leave. He knows our mind and plans, even before their expression in our brains. Indeed, we cannot even will for anything unless Allah wills.

28
PRESENT, FUTURE AND THE PAST ARE THE SAME TO HIM

Since He Himself is Absolute Time, therefore, present, future and past are also the one and the same thing to Him. He sees them all at the same time. Moreover, things change and decay with time. Only the 'Time' itself can be immortal. So Allah is Immortal, ever active, neither tires, nor sleeps. He is the Absolute Reality, and everything else is relative to Him.

29
WHAT IS HE LIKE?

The Qur'an tells, us that there is nothing like unto Him. He is unique in all respects: infinite in His attributes, indivisible whole, beyond our comprehension, the grand singularity who encompasses everything. Sura al-Ikhlas of the Holy Qur'an describes the personality of Allah *Subhana-Hu* in the following words,

قُلْ هُوَ اللّٰهُ اَحَدْ ۞ اَللّٰهُ الصَّمَدْ ۞ لَمْ يَلِدْ ۬ وَلَمْ يُوْلَدْ ۞ وَلَمْ يَكُنْ لَّهُ كُفُوًا اَحَدْ ۞

Proclaim (O! Man), He is Allah, the 'Ahad' (Alone, One and the only, the Grand Singularity); He is Allah, the 'Samad' (the Absolute, the Indivisible Whole, the Self Sufficient who depends on

none, while everything else depends on Him); He begets not, nor is He begotten (He is by Himself only) And there is absolutely none like unto Him (He is unique in all respects) [114(1-4)]

Thus it is absurd to say that He has a son, father or mother or that He saved mankind by sacrificing His own son. Even more absurd is idol worshipping and assigning partners to Him.

30
THE CREATION OF EVENTS

As described earlier, the physical world is a manifestation and manipulation of the time, space and energy attributes of Allah *Subhana-Hu*. Any event in the universe is essentially a function of these three attributes, i.e. $E = f(tse)$.

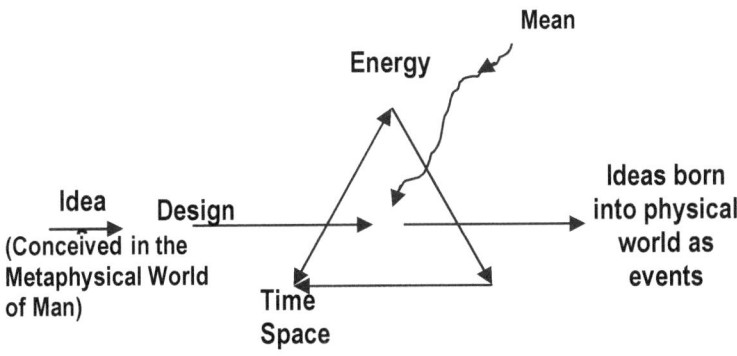

Fig: Trio of Time, Space and Energy causes events from ideas

After the conception of an idea in mind, it is translated into design for implementation. If Allah *Subhana-Hu* wills He provides the required time-space-energy inputs for the event to occur. Since the absolute and supreme mind is of Allah *Subhana-Hu* only, He is the primal cause of everything.

> ***To Allah belongs all things in the Heavens and Earth: Verily Allah is He (who is) free of all wants – worthy of all praises [31(26)]***
>
> ***And if all the trees on earth were pens, and all the oceans were ink, with seven oceans behind it to add to (its supply), yet would not the words of Allah (description of His creation in the writing) be exhausted; Lo! Allah is exalted in power, full of wisdom [31(27)]***

Part II

The Irrefutable Challenge of the Holy Qur'an to Science

31
THE GLORIOUS QUR'AN – A CHALLENGE

> "Verily this Qur'an is no less than a message to (all) the worlds. It (profits) to who ever among you wills to go straight". 81(27-28)

The Holy Qur'an is the eternal message of Allah *Subhana-Hu* to mankind, revealed to the last of the messengers of Allah, (peace be upon him), in Arabia more than fourteen centuries ago. It consolidates and completes the teachings of all the prophets of Allah who came before him. The miraculous qualities of this Book may be judged by its profound influence on the lives of its believers and the unrivalled impact it had on culture, science and technology latter on. Even the developments of western social institutions, welfare philosophy, science and technology are also indebted to the Qur'an, as it inherited them from the Muslims[6].

It is not a voluminous book, yet it has something to say on all subjects, from the big bang to the end of universe. A clear, concise and comprehensive Guidance, without contradiction or ambiguity, it is to guide man to the spiritual heights as well as the physical developments in this world.

Indeed it is unique in every respect. Its scope of guidance and the quality of message is never out of date. One can

---

[6] HAR Gibb "WHY Islam?", Lahore 1932, p 379. Mar quis Duggerir: Speech Delivered in India, London   Page Leopold Weiss "The Message of the Qur'an" Al-Andalus, Gibraltar, 1980

read it again and again without getting bored. It is the most revered and most acted upon book in the history of mankind, and as time passes, more and more people discover its riches and believe in it as the true revelation of Allah *Subhana-Hu,* for all times to come. If Islam today is the fastest growing religion, it is due to the Holy Qur'an only.

Its principal objective is to take with it the man to spiritual heights so that he may regain his lost paradise (جنت). But it is equally important for salvation in this world too. Qur'an is the proof of truth itself. It comes from the Creator of the universe, who challenge,

> ***And in case you are in doubt about what We have revealed on Our servant (Muhammad PBUH), then if you are right in your (doubt), produce just a chapter like it; And you may call all your supporters, except Allah. So if you can't do it, and sure enough you will not be able to do it, then save yourself from the (hell) fire whose fuel shall be (disbelieving) mankind and stones. It is prepared for the rejecters of the truth". [2 (23-24)]***

This challenge is repeated a number of times in the Holy Qur'an, for example, at 11(13) it says:

> **They accuse that he has forged it;**
> **Say! Then bring ten Suras like it;**
> ***And call upon whom you can, except Allah***
> ***If you are truthful***

And at 17(88) the Qur'an challenges,

> *If Mankind and the Jinns were together,*
> *To produce like of the Qur'an,*
> *They could never produce in like thereof,*
> *Even if they backed up one another*

This challenge, which has now stood for more than fourteen centuries, is a clear proof of the divine truth of the Holy Qur'an. There are a few truthful Christian scholars of Islam who also acknowledge this. For example Harry Gaylord Dorman in his book comments, "It (the Qur'an) is the literal revelation of God dictated to Muhammad by Jibrael, perfect in the every letter. It is an ever present miracle witnessing itself"[7].

Professor Arberry in his translation of the Holy Qur'an argues that, "Western misunderstandings of the Holy Qur'an are due to translations and the fact that the Western reader has not been sufficiently advised how to read the Holy Qur'an. He must get rid of the assumption that the Holy Qur'an is more or less like the Old Testament"[8]. Further he says, (p-x) "I have been at pains to study the intricate and richly valid rethym which – apart from the message itself – constitutes the Koran's undeniable claim to rank amongst the greatest literary masterpiece of mankind". (3)

---

[7] Harry Gaylord Dorman, "Towards Understanding Islam," 1948, New York, USA
[8] Arthur J. Arberry "The Koran Interpreted" pul. Oxford university Ress.... 1964.

32
THE QUR'AN AND SCIENCE

Dr. Maurice Bucaille a French national, out of his curiosity for different religions conducted research on the Bible and the Qur'an, from the perspective of modern scientific discoveries. His findings are published in his book, 'The Bible, The Qur'an and Science' ('La Bible, la Coran et, la Science'), published in 1979[9]. In its introduction (p vii), he writes,

> *As we shall see later on, the Qur'an deals with many subjects of interest to science, far more in fact than the Bible. There is no comparison between the limited number of Biblical statements which lead to a confrontation with science, and the profusion of subjects mentioned in the Qur'an that are of a scientific nature. None of the latter can be contested from a scientific point of view; this is the basic fact that emerges from our study.*

He goes on the write on page viii,

> *It was in a totally objective spirit, and without any preconceived ideas that I first examined the Qur'anic Revelation. I was looking for the degree of compatibility between the Qur'anic text and the data of modern science. I knew from translations that the Qur'an often made allusion to all sorts of natural phenomena, but I had only a summary knowledge of it. It was only when I examined the text very closely in*

---

[9] Maurice Bucaille, "The Bible, the Qur'an and Science" First published in France, translated & printed in 1979, Muslim Printing Press, Karachi

Arabic that I kept a list of them at the end of which I had to acknowledge the evidence in front of me: the Qur'an did not contain a single statement that was assailable from a modern scientific point of view.

About the Bible, Bucaille says,

I repeated the same test for the Old Testament and the Gospels, always preserving the same objective outlook. In the former, I did not even have to go beyond the first book, Genesis to find statements totally out of keeping with the cast-iron facts of modern science.

Toward the end of his book Bucaille concludes,

In view of the level of knowledge in Muhammad's day, it is inconceivable that many of the statements in the Qur'an which are connected with science could have been the work of a man. It is, moreover, perfectly legitimate, not only to regard the Qur'an as the expression of a Revelation, but also to award it a very special place, on account of the guarantee of authenticity it provides and the presence in it of scientific statements which, when studied today, appear as a challenge to explanation in human terms.

33
QUR'AN PROVIDES THE ANSWERS

Indeed Maurice Bucaille is correct in his view. Many questions which have bothered the greatest modern scientific minds about the universe are answered in the Qur'an. In simple clear precise and comprehensive way.

Some of these puzzles as pointed out by Stephen Hawking, the famous British physicist are, *"Is the universe actually infinite or just very large? And is it everlasting or just long-lived? How could our finite minds comprehend an infinite universe? Isn't it presumptuous of us even to make the attempt? Do we risk the fate of Prometheus, who in classical mythology stole fire from Zeus for human beings to use, and was punished for his temerity by being chained to a rock where an eagle picked at his liver? Despite this cautionary tale, I believe we can and should try to understand the universe. We have already made remarkable progress in understanding the cosmos, particularly in the last few years. We don't yet have a complete picture, but this may not be far off"*[10].

It is unfortunate that Stephen Hawking did not study the Holy Qur'an. Had he, as you will see later in this book, he would be surprised that it has already provided answers to many of his questions.

Unfortunately, western mind is mostly prejudiced, clouded by doubts and ignorance about Islam. They take Islam as one of the religions comparable to Christianity, Judaism, Hinduism, etc and associate it with the conduct of misguided Muslims, who don't really project the true spirit of Islam. Disillusioned by their own religions, some of them out rightly reject all religions. In this regard, the comments of physicist Paul Davies reveal the mindset of modern western thinkers,

> *The world's major religions, founded on received wisdom and dogma, are rooted in the past and do not*

---

[10] Stephen Hawking "The Universe in a Nutshell" p 69, London

cope easily with changing times. Hastily discovered flexibility has enabled Christianity to incorporate some new features of modern thought, to the extent that today's Church leaders might well have appeared heretical to a Victorian; yet any comprehensive philosophy based on ancient concepts faces a hard task in adapting to the space age. As a result, many disillusioned believers have turned to 'fringe' religions that seem more in tune with the era of Star Wars and microchips. The huge rise in popularity of cults associated with UFOs, ESP, spirit contacts, scientology, transcendental meditation and other technology-based beliefs testifies to the continued persuasiveness of faith dogma in a superficially rational and scientific society. For although these eccentric ideas have a scientific veneer, they are unashamedly irrational — 'cults of unreason', to use Christopher Evans's phrase from his book of the same title (Panther 1974). People turn to them not for intellectual enlightenment but for spiritual comfort in a harsh and uncertain world.[11]

On the same subject he further says, *"If the church is largely ignored today it is not that science has finally won its age-old battle with religion but because it had so radically reoriented our society that the believer's perspective of the world now seems irrelevant".*

Alas! Muslims have badly failed to bring the great wisdom of the Holy Qur'an to the notice of the western world. Had they done so, views of Paul Davies and other scholars like him would have been different about the revealed

---

[11] Paul Davies, "God and the New Physics" p 2, 1983, Simon & Schuster, New York

religions, is at least about Islam. Had they studied the Qur'an objectively, their perception about it would have been quite different. As noted already, this realism is evident from the findings of the French doctor Maurice Bucaille, who could not find a single discrepancy between science and Qur'an. How could he? It is a revelation from Allah *Subhana-Hu,* the sole creator of the universe, and is preserved for all times exactly as it was revealed to His messenger (PBUH).

The Holy Qur'an itself is the proof of its truth. As we ponder over it, puzzled we ask, how could a book revealed more than 1,400 years ago in Arabia, describe some of the greatest scientific discoveries of the modern age so precisely? Moreover, the mathematical arrangement of its letters, words, ayaat, and chapters is simply mind boggling. In the following chapters we will look into some of these great truths.

However, readers should appreciate that the Holy Qur'an is not a book of professional details. It only lays down the fundamentals precepts. Even in religious matters, the details were left to the messenger of Allah (PBUH) to explain. In scientific matters they are left for man to discover and explain. Nevertheless, for any honest scientific mind, it is surprising how it leads science in the basic truths about nature. One wonders how could Muhammad (PBUH) state the mysteries of nature so accurately and arrange his book in stupefying mathematical arrangement. If he was not the messenger of God, then he must have been the greatest scientist and mathematician of all times. In the following pages you will judge for yourself.

34
THE FOUNDATION OF THE SCIENTIFIC METHOD

The scientific method is considered to be of fundamental importance for the development of science and the understanding of nature. Basically it lays stress on logical analysis and empirical evidence. The Holy Qur'an has emphasized the significance of sound argument supported by the physical verification and continuous research. Earlier, Greek science believed only in logic. In fact Greek philosophers condescended experiment and physical verification as they thought it an affront to human intellect. In contrast the Holy Qur'an teaches us to reach truth through analysis, research, observation, measurement and verification by performing physical experimentation. In this respect the general principle given in the Holy Qur'an is, قُلْ هَاتُوا بُرْهَانَكُمْ إِنْ كُنْتُمْ صَادِقِينَ **"Say, bring out clear evidence if you are right."** Besides, the Holy Qur'an lays great stress on acquiring knowledge, so that man may develop insight of the unknown based on what is known. It asks, **"Are those who know and those who know not, equal?" 39(9).** It regards wisdom as the greatest asset of man, as evidenced clearly in ayat 249 of sura al-Baqara. **"The one who is bestowed with wisdom, he has been blessed with great good".** In his love of knowledge, the Holy Prophet (PBUH) used to frequently pray, **"O Allah! show me the reality of things, as they are – O Allah! Increase me in knowledge".**

As for the method to reach to the truth the following commands from the Qur'an provide sound guidelines for scientific research.

مَا تَرَى فِي خَلْقِ الرَّحْمَنِ مِنْ تَفَاوُتٍ ۖ فَارْجِعِ الْبَصَرَ هَلْ تَرَى مِنْ فُطُورٍ ۞ ثُمَّ ارْجِعِ الْبَصَرَ كَرَّتَيْنِ يَنْقَلِبْ إِلَيْكَ الْبَصَرُ خَاسِئًا وَهُوَ حَسِيرٌ ۞

> "You will see no flaw in the creations of the most Compassionate. So turn your gaze again. Do you see any flaw? Then turn your gaze again and again (go on searching). Your vision will come back to you exhausted, in a state worn out. (You will not discover any flaw in nature)"
> 67(3-4).

In this ayat the command, *"Turn your gaze again and again"* is an order from the Creator, that mankind must discover the reality by repeated verification and continuous research. For believers, this command forms the goal to make scientific research the essence of their culture.

For empirical evidence the Holy Qur'an asked its followers to travel on earth and look for the signs of Allah in their natural environment. It commands,

قُلْ سِيرُوا فِي الْأَرْضِ فَانْظُرُوا كَيْفَ بَدَأَ الْخَلْقَ ثُمَّ اللَّهُ يُنْشِئُ النَّشْأَةَ الْآخِرَةَ ۚ إِنَّ اللَّهَ عَلَىٰ كُلِّ شَيْءٍ قَدِيرٌ ۞

> "Tell them (O Messenger of Allah!) to travel on earth. Thereby look into how Allah originated things the first time. Then think, how Allah recreates them. Indeed Allah has the power to do everything". sura al-Ankaboot, 20.

As a result of these and other such commands in the Holy Qur'an, Muslim scientists founded their science on the basis of sound knowledge, physical verification, research and experimentation, which is now known as the scientific method. It is unfortunate that over the ages when Muslim societies degenerated, that history has been distorted and credit due to Muslims for scientific development has been largely misappropriated. Irrespective however, the evidence of the Holy Qur'an exists in its original form, wherefrom every just person can deduce the truth and correct their perception of Islam.

35
HOW DID THE UNIVERSE BEGIN?

The scientific community now believes that our universe came into existence some fifteen billion years ago. However, before 1950 the generally accepted theory about of the universe was that it had always been like that. This hypothesis was known as the steady state universe theory. The postulate of an eternal universe without beginning or end suggested no need for God either. Unsurprisingly, it was quite popular with atheists. British scientist, Fred Hoyle was one of its great advocates. He writes, "I find myself forced to assure that the Nature of Universe requires continuous creation – the perpetual bringing into being of new background natural matter that already exists creates new matter to appear"[12]. However idea of perpetual universe was totally against the Holy Qur'an, which argues in favour of a Supreme Creator. According to it, permanence is only for Allah, all else is transient. Everything in the Universe was created by Him. Nothing

---

[12] Fred Hoyle, "The Nature of the Universe", pp 109-110, Pelican, 1963

apart from Him can be perpetual. The universe must, therefore have a beginning. The Qur'an categorically declares,

اَلْحَمْدُ لِلّٰهِ الَّذِىْ خَلَقَ السَّمٰوٰتِ وَالْاَرْضَ وَجَعَلَ الظُّلُمٰتِ وَ النُّوْرَ ڎ ثُمَّ الَّذِيْنَ كَفَرُوْا بِرَبِّهِمْ يَعْدِلُوْنَ ۞

All praise be to Allah, who created all the heavens and the earth (universe), and made the darkness and the light; yet those who reject faith, hold (others) in parallel with their Sustainer [6(1)]

It is evident from this and many similar ayaat of the Holy Qur'an, that the universe is not eternal but a created reality. It must have a beginning, and shall see an end too. Similarly the phenomena of light and darkness are not eternal, but created entities. In the order of priority, ayat 6(1) shows that darkness was the first, and light came later.

Belief in an Absolute Creator automatically means that the universe cannot be eternal. So the steady state universe theory must be false. Nothing that is created can possess perpetual existence. Immortality can only be for the Absolute Creator.

Modern science has emerged as a witness to the truth of the Holy Qur'an. In 1960, the discovery of symmetry in background radiation all over space brought about a change in the theories about creation of universe. The upshot of this research eventually was the big bang theory that changed the conception of a universe with eternal life in favour of a universe which had a beginning, and eventually, will have an end. This is now the accepted scientific hypothesis about the creation and life of the universe. The scientific world now believes that the universe indeed has been created. About fifteen billion years ago, the universe burst into existence out of nothing, with an awesome explosion, popularly known as the 'big bang'. According to physicist Paul Davies, *"There are many strands of evidence to support this astonishing theory. Whether one accepts all the details or not, the essential hypothesis – that there was some sort of creation – seems from the scientific point of view, compelling"*[13].

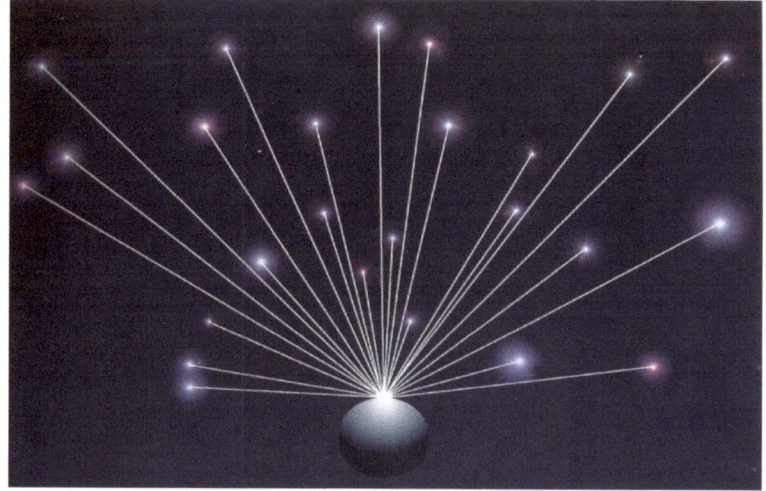

On the same subject the famous British physicist Stephen Hawking says, *"The observation that we have all made, that the sky at night is dark, is very important. It implies that the universe cannot have existed forever in the state we see today. Something must have happened in the past to make the stars light up a finite time ago, which means that the light from very distant stars has not had time to*

---

[13]   Paul Davies: God and the New Physics, penguin Books – 1987.

reach us yet. This would explain why the sky at night isn't glowing in every direction.

If the stars had just been sitting there forever, why did they suddenly light up a few billion years ago? What was the clock that told them it was time to shine? As we've seen, this puzzled those philosophers, much like Immanuel Kant, who believed that the universe had existed forever"[14].

Note the observation of Dr Hawking about darkness and light that in the process of creation darkness was the first in order of priority. Light came later. Now think over again in the ayat 6(1) quoted already, *"He made darkness and light"*.

It would probably have surprised Hawking, Davies and other likeminded western scientists that the Holy Qur'an had repeatedly stressed that **"Allah has created everything"**. The universe is no exception. It was also created by Him. So "Steady State Theory" emphasizing perpetual universe could never be right.

The Big Bang

The Holy Qur'an not only points out, that the universe is a finite creation, but also how it was created. We need only to reflect into the following ayat to figure this out,

بَدِيْعُ السَّمٰوٰتِ وَالْاَرْضِ ۖ وَاِذَا قَضٰى اَمْرًا فَاِنَّمَا يَقُوْلُ لَهُ كُنْ فَيَكُوْنُ ۞

(Allah is the) Originator of the heaven and the earth (universe). When He decrees a thing, He says unto it only "Be" and it is [2(117)]

---

14   Stephen Hawking. "The Universe in a Nutshell" - London

On the same subject ayaat (81-82) of sura Yaseen say;

اَوَلَيْسَ الَّذِىْ خَلَقَ السَّمٰوٰتِ وَالْاَرْضَ بِقٰدِرٍ عَلٰى اَنْ يَّخْلُقَ مِثْلَهُمْ ؕ بَلٰى ۪ وَهُوَ الْخَلّٰقُ الْعَلِيْمُ ؕ اِنَّمَآ اَمْرُهٗٓ اِذَآ اَرَادَ شَيْـًٔا اَنْ يَّقُوْلَ لَهٗ كُنْ فَيَكُوْنُ ؕ

Does not He Who created the heavens and earth (universe), has the power to create the like thereof? Of course He does! He is All knowing Supreme Creator. Whenever He intends a thing, He needs only to say: Be! And it is there. [36 (81-82)]

Thus as Allah intended to create the universe, He simply said "Be" and it was there...a big bang. From nothingness, came along the universe this way.

It is amazing how a man in Arabia, over fourteen hundred years ago could assert the creation and origin of the universe in such clear terms. It could only be explained as an inspiration from the Creator Himself. One wonders, if modern man really believes in the sudden creation of universe with a big bang what then prevents him from believing in the Holy Qur'an, which was the first to point out this reality.

36
WHY THE UNIVERSE AND EVERYTHING IN IT?

With the overwhelming acceptance of the theory of big bang, science at last found the answer to the long standing question of how the universe began. However, the question, why the universe? is beyond the comprehension of science. In this respect science and philosophy still have a lot to learn from the Holy Qur'an.

The Holy Qur'an exposes the fundamental law of Divine purpose behind everything that we may discover. Accordingly, the universe as a whole is not the meaningless outcome of an accident, but is a planned design of Allah *Subhana-Hu*. As discussed below it is the integral part of His master plan of the creation of Man. As for the universe, it lays down on the rule,

$$\text{خَلَقَ السَّمٰوٰتِ وَالْاَرْضَ بِالْحَقِّ}$$

"Allah created the heavens and earth (universe) in accordance with a true purpose" [64(3)].

The same theme is stressed in ayat 21(16),

$$\text{وَمَا خَلَقْنَا السَّمَآءَ وَالْاَرْضَ وَمَا بَيْنَهُمَا لٰعِبِيْنَ}$$

And We have not created the heavens and the earth, (Universe) and all that is in between them in play [21(16)]

These ayaat clearly point out that creation of the universe with everything in it, big small or small, is an objective reality. Nothing is purposeless in the universe. Everything fulfils the design of Allah *Subhana-Hu*. Thus the aim of science should also be to discover the Divine purpose of creation in everything.

As pointed out earlier, according to the Holy Qur'an, the fundamental design basis of the universe is Man, He is the very reason for creation of it. In this respect, the Holy

Qur'an repeatedly declares, "*Allah has created the heavens and the earth, and everything in them for him only.*" For example, ayat 16 of sura An-Nahl announces,

وَسَخَّرَ لَكُمُ الَّيْلَ وَالنَّهَارَ ۙ وَالشَّمْسَ وَالْقَمَرَ ۭ وَالنُّجُوْمُ مُسَخَّرٰتٌۢ بِاَمْرِهٖ ۭ اِنَّ فِيْ ذٰلِكَ لَاٰيٰتٍ لِّقَوْمٍ يَّعْقِلُوْنَ ۞

And He has subjected the night and day and the sun and the moon to be of service unto you and the stars made subservient by His Command. Lo! Herein are portents for the people who have sense [16 (12)]

The law that everything in the universe is made for mankind implies that man is not a product of the universe but the very reason for it. This exposes the fallacy of the evolutionists who claim that man is a product of the universe, and has evolved over a long period of time, as a result of various accidents of nature. In contrast, the guidance of the Holy Qur'an is that every bit of the universe, from sub-atomic particles to the great clusters of stars and galaxies, is created to serve man. This also provides direction to science that it should be for Man only.

A purposeful universe means that creation of everything is in accordance with a pre-designed programme. Thus the Holy Qur'an states,

مَا خَلَقْنَا السَّمٰوٰتِ وَالْاَرْضَ وَمَا بَيْنَهُمَآ اِلَّا بِالْحَقِّ وَاَجَلٍ مُّسَمًّى ۭ وَالَّذِيْنَ كَفَرُوْا عَمَّآ اُنْذِرُوْا مُعْرِضُوْنَ ۞

We have not created the heaven and the earth (universe) and all that lies in between them but with a true Design and

that also is for a pre-programmed term;
But those who reject faith, turn away
whereof they are warned. [46(3)]

It is not surprising that modern science has emerged as an adherent to this truth of the Holy Qur'an. It is based upon the fact that universe is an integrated, purposeful and logical creation.

Thus answer to the questions, 'why', 'how, and 'where' about the universe should be sought with reference to man, who is the primary objective of creation. Science should be directed to discover how things are made to serve this purpose. Its own purpose should also be to serve the good of man.

37
THE EXPANSION OF THE UNIVERSE

That the universe has been expanding since its beginning, is a proud discovery of modern science. According to renowned British physicist Stephen Hawking it is a great intellectual revolution (12). Russian scientist I.D. Novikov calls it the greatest reasoning of the human intellect (13). It should surprise both of them that this fact was first pointed out in the Holy Qur'an.

In the landmark scientific discovery of 1927, American astronomer Edwin Hubble, noting the difference of red shifts in stars due to Doppler Effect, presented the hypothesis that galaxies are receding away at very high speeds and thus the universe is actually expanding rapidly instead of being static. Later observations proved that galaxies are also moving apart to some distant destination.

The rate of its expansion at the farthest boundaries may be close to the speed of light. It is expanding like a balloon expanding under pressure.

Fig: Universe is expanding like a balloon being filled with air

In this regard the explanation by Paul Davies sums up modern scientific thought, "Because the distant galaxies recede faster than the nearby ones, the gaps between the galaxies also expand, so in fact every galaxy is moving away from every other one. This is the famous 'expanding universe'. The pattern of galactic dispersal would appear very much the same from wherever in the cosmos you looked"[15].

About the reasons for this expansion, Davies further writes,

The expanding universe accords very well with modern thinking on the nature of space, time and motion. Albert Einstein, who carries the same status in the scientific community as St. Paul does among Christians, revolutionized our conception of these matters with his mind-boggling theory of relativity. Although it has taken sixty years for Einstein's space-warps and time-warps to impinge on the popular imagination, physicists have long accepted his ideas of curved space-time as an explanation of gravity.

---

[15] Paul Davies "God and the Modern Physics"

The force of gravity powers all large-scale cosmic phenomena. In objects of astronomical size, gravity far outweighs all other forces such as magnetism or electricity. It shapes the galaxies and controls the intergalactic motions. When it comes to explaining the expanding Universe, gravity is the key.

He further explains,
Einstein argued convincingly that gravity stretches or distorts space and time, and the idea can be checked directly by watching the sun's gravity bend star beams that graze its surface. The sky behind the sun appears from Earth to be slightly, but distinctly, bent. The elasticity of time can also be demonstrated, most directly by flying clocks in space. Time runs faster in the gravity-free environment up there than it does on the Earth's surface.

If the sun can stretch space so can the galaxy, which is made of many suns. So rather than thinking of the galaxies as moving apart through space, astronomers prefer to think of the space between the galaxies as stretching. If intergalactic space is being 'inflated', then each day every galaxy will find itself with more and more elbow room. In that way the universe expands, without having to expand into some external void.

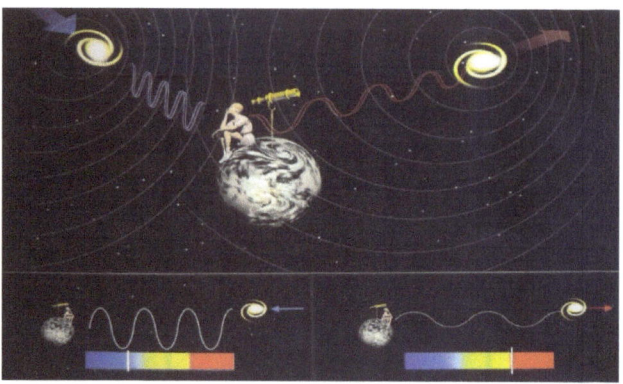

Fig: Show Space being squeezed or stretched due to gravity

Let us now listen to another famous twentieth century physicist on this subject: this is English Professor Stephen Hawking of Cambridge University,

> *The discovery of the expansion of the universe was one of the great intellectual revolutions of the twentieth century. It came as a total surprise, and it completely changed the discussion of the origin of the universe. If the galaxies are moving apart, they must have been closer together in the past. From the present rate of expansion, we can estimate that they must have been very close together indeed ten to fifteen billion years ago[16].*

---

[16] Stephen Hawking, "The Universe in a Nutshell", London

Fig: Expanding galaxies in an expanding universe

The scientific significance of the discovery that the universe is expanding and not static is immense. The Russian scientist I.D. Novikov has this to say, *"And at last in 1929, the American astronomer Edwin Hubble, having analysed the reality of many observations, established the fact of the expansion of the Universe. In this way the global evolution of the Universe was proved. This discovery became one of the greatest achievements of human reasoning"*[17].

Indeed it is a great tribute to scientists over the past centuries that endeavoured so hard in their dedication to resolving this mystery of nature. But what would you say about someone who told you fourteen hundred years ago, that the universe is expanding since its beginning? The greatest scientist of them all? A great visionary, or an inspired man from the Creator Himself? Indeed, long before modern science, the Prophet of Allah, Muhammad

---

[17] ID Novikov "Evolution of the Universe" Cambridge University Press, 1989

(PBUH), presented this reality very eloquently and clearly. It was revealed to him.

وَالسَّمَآءَ بَنَيْنَٰهَا بِأَيْدٍ وَإِنَّا لَمُوسِعُونَ ۝

And We built the Heaven (Universe) with (the Twist of) Our Hands, and We surely are expanding it [51 (47)] (Translation by Abdullah Yusuf Ali)

And it is We Who have built the Universe with (Our Creative) Power; and, verily, it is We Who are expanding it [51(47)] (Translated by Leopold Muhammad Asad (Austrian new Muslim)

Let's look closely at the meaning of this particular ayat in the two most widely accepted translations of the Qur'an. Yusuf Ali uses a slightly more graphic language. Accordingly, the Holy Qur'an did not tell only about the reality of the "Expansion of the Universe" but also pointed out the reason behind it. The statement "We built the heaven with the Twist of Our Hands" implies that the big bang push must have a spinning motion. Thus according to the law of conservation of momentum, the universe is not only expanding but also rotating since its beginning due to the Divine Twist imparted at its origin.

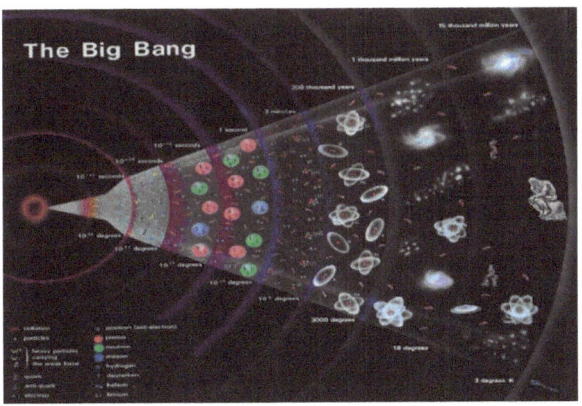

Fig: The big bang and the expanding universe

It is a wonder how Muhammad (PBUH) could assert so unambiguously that universe was expanding if he was not inspired by the creator of the universe Himself. Alas, many still do not believe in him!

38
A DYNAMIC UNIVERSE

Let us now consider another breathtaking aspect of the universe – it is the dynamic nature of the universe. Not very long ago, the general scientific belief was that the world is a fixed place with stars hanging overhead in the heavenly dome. According to Novikov, *"The idea of the static universe seemed so attractive that even Einstein did not believe his equations and began to change them."* Modern discoveries prove however, that the universe is an extremely dynamic place, where the process of creation, destruction and recreation is going on at all times. On completing their maturity, stars explode and new stars and planets take birth from this debris. Thus creation of the new worlds and demise of the old ones is an ongoing process in the universe. On this dynamics of universe, Novikov writes further[18]

> Nowadays the idea of the evolution of the Universe appears quite natural and even necessary, but this has not always been so. Like any great scientific idea, it took a lot of shaping and struggling through before it eventually triumphed in science. Today, the evolution of the Universe is a scientific fact, substantiated by many astrophysical observations and supported by the solid theoretical basis of all physics.
>
> From today's point of view, that anti-evolutionary prejudice, that search for static solutions to cosmological equations appears to be wrong even in principle because the evolution of all those heavenly bodies and systems, which earlier seemed to shine constantly and move steadily along circular orbits, has now been firmly established.
>
> Today, we observe violent explosive and evolutionary processes in such gigantic systems as the galaxies too. The matter constituting the galaxies is being gradually reprocessed via nuclear reactions occurring in stars. Hydrogen is being converted into helium, and into heavier elements afterwards.

According to C. R. Kitchin[19]

The births of stars, and more particularly the birth of the solar systems, are thus intimately connected with

---

[18] ID Novikov, ibid, p 3
[19] CR Kitchin "Journey to the End of the Universe", USA

the death of stars, the one rising phoenix-like from the ashes of the other. Numerous supernovae must have occurred between the formation of the galaxy and that of the solar system in order to build up the heavy elements forming the Earth and ourselves. It is likely that the collapse of the cloud could have been initiated by a pressure wave from a supernova. Finally, as we have just seen, a supernova may well have occurred within a few light years of the nascent Earth and remainder of the planetary system.

Fig: Death of a nearby star

Figure above show supernovae explosions and formation of new solar systems from the resulting debris

From these views of the scientists we can appreciate the significance the discovery that universe is not a static entity but a highly dynamic one. Indeed it is a tribute to science that after millennia of observation and analysis it discovered this attribute in the universe. But what would you say if you were told that the Holy Qur'an had already made this fact clear?! The Supreme Creator, after having created once, did not assign Himself to redundancy. He is infinitely active as revealed in sura Ar-Rahman, **"Every day is a Day of new Splendour for Him" 55(29).**

At 83 (13), it is revealed that the process of creation and recreation is a continuous process, **"Indeed He (Allah) keeps creating and re-creating since the very beginning".**

Allah's words are the absolute truth. The ayat above applies even at the heart of the atom, thus, radioactive decay in the atomic nucleus is the source of creation of new elements. Similarly activity at the galactic level is constantly throwing up brand new heavenly worlds.

Indeed every moment is a manifestation of the splendour of our Creator. It is not a surprise at all great truths of science about universal bear witness to the truth of the Book of Allah, the Holy Qur'an. Sadly though, even then a majority of people are ignorant of it.

39
THE JOURNEY OF THE SUN IN THE HEAVENS

When science considered the sun as a stationary body in heaven, even great minds like Kepler and Galileo believed that. But new scientific discoveries of the 20th century have changed this monotonous view about sun. It has been confirmed that it is travelling in space at a speed of about 200 miles per second (covering 6.3 billion miles a year, which is 66 times the distance between the earth and the sun). Novikov states this fact, *"It has been established that the Sun orbits around the centre of our Galaxy with a speed of 250 km/sec".*

It may surprise some that the Holy Qur'an had already revealed that the sun is not stationary, but a traveller in space. sura Yasin, ayat 38 says,

> ***The sun keeps on running on its course to its predetermined destination. That is the measurement fixed for it by the Almighty, All-Knowledgeable (Allah) [36(38)]***

Fig: Journey of the sun through space

Not much is known about the nature of this movement. Is it a straight line, or a swing around some super orbit? Nor has the sun's final destination been discovered yet. However, it is a perilous journey through the heavens, which houses billions of galaxies, and trillions upon trillions of stars, planets and other bodies. The possibility of a crash cannot be ruled out, which will be its doomsday.

The point however is, how could the Holy Qur'an have pointed out the continuous motion of the sun in space, if it were not a revelation from the Creator of the Universe?

40
THE UNIVERSE WAS A CLOSED MASS IN THE BEGINNING

On the subject of the creation of universe, science discovered that in the beginning everything inside the universe was compressed together. All matter and all energy were originally in the form of an extremely high density primordial soup, which latter upon expansion and cooling, formed into heavenly worlds. All these uncountable billions of galaxies with trillions of stars and planets inside them, were once close together as a single mass.

Says Novikov, *"Friedman's solution when extrapolated to the past, lead formally to the initial state of infinite density"*[20]. Thus the whole of matter and energy, now comprising billions of galaxies, each consisting of trillions of stars, was concentrated, some 15 billion years ago, into a single point of infinite density, called a 'singularity'. It is postulated that the density of this matter, immediately after the big bang took place, could be over 10^{93} g/cm^3, i.e. infinitely high.

Again, it may surprise some that centuries earlier, the Holy Qur'an had disclosed in clear terms that in the beginning all the heavens and the earth were together, as a single mass. Consider the following thought provoking ayat below,

---

[20] Novikov, ibid, p 93

أَوَلَمْ يَرَ الَّذِيْنَ كَفَرُوْٓا اَنَّ السَّمٰوٰتِ وَالْاَرْضَ كَانَتَا رَتْقًا فَفَتَقْنٰهُمَا

Have not the ones who reject the faith (in Islam) seen (discovered), that the heavens and the earth were together (as one unit mass); Then We caused them asunder? (Al-Ambia, 30)

The beginning phrase of this ayat, "Have not those who reject the faith seen..." is also an astonishing prophecy. It is a prediction that this great discovery will be made not by the believers, but by the non-believers. Alas! Even then they do not believe in the divine origin of the Holy Qur'an.

41
EQUILIBRIUM AND STABILITY IN THE UNIVERSE

Mystery surrounds how order emerged out of the initial chaos of big bang? How did primordial matter and energy that came out of the big bang settle down to give birth to individual stars and other heavenly bodies? This is in violation of the second law of thermodynamics which states that if left at its own, a system will degenerate into disorder unless corrected by external means. But in the case of the universe we see an orderly world emerging out of the chaotic blast of the big bang. How did it happen? Does the Holy Qur'an provide guidance on this question, that really goes to the heart of the existence of our universe today and which science has been unable to answer thus far? Indeed it does! But before that let us review what modern science has to say about this.

It has been recently discovered that equilibrium and stability in the universe had begun to prevail only after it had exceeded certain critical dimensions after the occurrence of the big bang. Initially, there was intense pressure and temperature in the primordial substance that blew out of the big bang, millions of times more than what prevails on the sun. As it was expanding, the universe, much more tiny than what we find now, was also cooling down. After it had expanded beyond a certain critical limit, perhaps due to perturbation in the rate of its expansion, matter began to amass at various places in separate cloud-like globules of gases. These gaseous globules on further cooling turned into primary material for the creation of stars. Thus, expansion was critical in attaining balance and equilibrium in the universe.

Scientific findings on this question have been summed up by Paul Davies in the following words,

> *In the expanding universe, the cosmic material comes under the influence of the cosmological gravitational field. We know that, given an external supply of energy, order can be created in one system at the expense of disorder in another. Thus the flux of heat and light from the sun generates the highly complex order of the Earth's biosphere, but only by sacrificing irreversibly the limited fuel resources of the solar core. In the same way, an expanding Universe can generate order in the cosmic material.*[21]

Thus science has arrived at the conclusion that order in the universe was conditional to its expansion. As it expanded,

---

[21] Paul Davies "God and the New Physics", p 50

order and stability started prevailing within it. This is truly an amazing discovery that adds to our understanding of the evolution of our beginning. But what will you say, if you were told that this incredible fact was first revealed in the Holy Qur'an fourteen hundred years ago? Will you believe it? Indeed the Holy Qur'an had revealed this truth in clear words much before science. It says,

اَلشَّمْسُ وَالْقَمَرُ بِحُسْبَانٍ ۞ وَالنَّجْمُ وَالشَّجَرُ يَسْجُدَانِ ۞ وَالسَّمَآءَ رَفَعَهَا وَوَضَعَ الْمِيْزَانَ ۞

The sun and the moon operate according to definite mathematical arrangement; (likewise) the stars (in the heaven), and plants (on earth), prostrate before Allah (obey His laws). And as for the Heaven (universe), (Allah) raised it high all over and established balance in it, thereof. [55(5-7)]

In this revolutionary ayat *"(Allah) raised heaven all over and established order therein"* points to the scene of the early universe. First of all it means that in the beginning universe must have been close together in a transient chaotic state. At the same time it was opening up also. Order in the universe began to prevail only after it had expanded beyond certain limits. This is what science has now discovered.

How could anybody have made such a startling statement even a hundred years ago? Even the best scientists then believed then that the universe had always been there. Indeed, only the Creator who revealed the Qur'an to his prophet Muhammad (PBUH) could expose such a fact about the universe so clearly and comfortably.

Will you still not believe?

42
PRIMORDIAL SMOKY STUFF

One of the more important discoveries about the early history of the universe is that long after its creation, for billions of years, the universe remained in the form of a high temperature smoky substance of light elements, predominantly hydrogen. This has been confirmed by modern instruments such as the Hubble telescope.

According to Carl Sagan, *"at the beginning of the universe, there were no galaxies, stars or planets, no life or civilization, merely a uniform radiant fireball filling all space"*[22].

"What we see are millions and millions of galaxies of various shapes and sizes formed afterwards from the collection and cooling of the earlier primordial smoky stuff. On its accumulation in large chunks, it started compressing under the gravitational pull and in this process got very hot also. As it got further compressed and heated, atomic fusion reactions started in their core as the factory to produce immense heat and light, and also heavier elements of matter. Thus the primordial smoke of immense volume turned into trillions of stars. Figure below show early stages of formation of galaxies from the original smoky stuff".

---

[22] Carl Sagan "Cosmos", p 33, Abacus, 1995

While describing the early universe, Novikov says, *"Clearly, at the epoch such high density, neither stars, nor any other celestial bodies existed. The expanding matter was, most probably, almost perfectly homogeneous. Later with expansion perturbations occurred in the expanding smoky stuff, which resulted into large gaseous clusters; which in turn over time formed galaxies, thereby condensed to from stars and planets"*[23]

---

[23] Novikov, ibid, p 95

Must it surprise you that way before modern science, the Holy Qur'an, had informed us in clear terms that the early universe consisted entirely of smoke? It had revealed thus,
ثُمَّ اسْتَوَى اِلَى السَّمَآءِ وَهِيَ دُخَانٌ *"Then He (Allah) tuned to the Heaven and it was smoke" 41(11).*
The question is how could Muhammad (PBUH) talk so authoritatively about such complex scientific matters concerning the early universe, if he was not inspired by the Creator of the worlds?

Will you even then not believe in the divine origin of Holy Qur'an?

43
THE UNIVERSE IS ROTATING

Let's now look into another great discovery, of modern science that universe is not only expanding but it is also rotating. A couple of centuries ago man thought earth was the only world, but over the last few hundred years, scientific discoveries have extended the vision to the infinite expanse of the universe. Science has now discovered that billions of stars and galaxies in the universe revolve on their orbits with great harmony. Stars, planets and satellites also rotate around their own axes. So after centuries of research and observation, it is now concluded that the universe with everything is rotating relative each other.

The earth, for instance rotates around its own axis at a mean velocity of about 1,670 km/hour. (A bullet has an average velocity of only 1800 km/hour). Besides its rotation on its own axis, the earth also revolves around the sun at a speed of about 108,000 km/hour – almost 60 times the velocity of a bullet. If it could be possible to design a vehicle of such speed, it would be able to go around the world in 22 minutes!

It has further been discovered that as systems increase in size, their velocity also increases. For example, the solar system as a whole revolves around the centre of the galaxy at a velocity of 720,000 km/hour. The velocity of the Milky Way galaxy, on its orbit in space along with its some 200 billion solar systems, is about 950,000 km/hour.

Fig: An image of a rotating galaxy

The tiny electrons in an atom are likewise rotating around the nucleus of the atom close to the spaced of light. It is truly amazing that there is hardly a body in the universe that excepts this rule. Just to add to the suspense, all big and small systems generally rotate anti-clockwise, which is the same direction in which the pilgrims circle around the Bait-Ullah in Makkah.

These are indeed great scientific discoveries of the twentieth century, but what would you say about the Holy Qur'an, which over fourteen centuries ago had already pointed out to this great reality of nature **"that whole of the universe rotates; infect rotation is in the very nature of things"**!

The Holy Qur'an announced clearly that rotation is an inbuilt attribute in the nature of the universe. Ayat 86(11) is testimonial to this truth,(والسّماء ذات الرّجع) **"As for the Heaven (Universe), rotation is its inbuilt nature" 86 (11).**

According to this Qur'anic revelation, every heavenly body must possess an inherent and natural rotation. We can see that moons revolve around their planets on their orbits; planets around the stars; the stars revolve in their respective orbits in the galaxies; and galaxies too, in turn revolve around their own centre of gravities; and so too are the electrons in a constant state of motion around the nuclei inside the atoms.

Ayat 21 of sura al-Ambia informs us of that is this grand system of rotation each one follows a specific orbit for it.

وَهُوَ الَّذِىْ خَلَقَ الَّيْلَ وَالنَّهَارَ وَالشَّمْسَ وَالْقَمَرَ ۚ كُلٌّ فِىْ فَلَكٍ يَّسْبَحُوْنَ ۝

And Allah is the one who has created (the cycle of) night and day, And the Sun and the Moon; All (heavenly bodies) float on their orbits. [21(33)]

It is astounding to imagine a human being talking about these extremely advanced and complex scientific matters about the nature, origin and function of the universe at a time which incidentally the western scholars have labelled the Dark Ages, when the knowledge of man was exceedingly limited. Far from an accurate assessment of the heavens, in those days he knew very little even about the earth. How could the Qur'an then, lay the fantastic claim, *"All (heavenly bodies) float in their orbits",* if it was not inspired by the Creator Himself? To this day, modern science cannot allege any falsification in this simple worded and straight forward scientific claim by the Holy Qur'an.

Will you not still believe in the Holy Qur'an?

44
THE INFINITENESS OF CREATION

Discoveries of modern science show the universe to be infinite in its expanse and its secrets are almost entirely unexposed. It was with this realization that Newton is reported to have confessed, *"I am like a small child playing with pebbles on the shore. A deep sea lies ahead of me, yet to discover."*

And on this issue Hawking asks, *"Is the universe actually infinite or just very large? And is it everlasting or just long-lived? How could our finite minds comprehend an infinite universe? Isn't it presumptuous of us even to make the attempt? Do we risk the fate of Prometheus, who in classical mythology stole fire from Zeus for human beings to use, and was punished for his temerity by being chained to a rock where an eagle picked at his liver?"*[24]

When the Qur'an was being revealed, man's world was extremely restricted, but at that time, in a mind boggling revelation the Qur'an announced the infiniteness of the creation of Allah *Subhana-Hu,* **"(O Muhammad) tell to the world, If oceans were the ink with which to write the Words of my Lord, these will not be enough, even if We brought similar quantity (of ink) to replenish it"** **18 (109).**

A much more recent story, narrated by President Ronald Reagan in a speech reflects man's inability to comprehend this reality, already exposed hundreds of years ago by the Holy Qur'an: In 1899, Charles Duell, the Commissioner of

---

[24] Hawking, Nutshell, p 69

the US Patents Office, sent his resignation to President McKinley, suggesting that 'everything that could be invented has been invented'! He urged the closing down of the patents office therefore.

Only in this modern age of discovery, can one grasp the depth of this revelation. Now when science informs us of a universe comprising of billions of galaxies, each housing trillions of stars, one can appreciate that all the oceans could indeed be insufficient to write details of the works of our Rabb.

Thus Qur'an taught that there is no limit to knowledge. Scientific endeavours will exhaust, but the works of Allah *Subhana-Hu* will always remain awaiting discovery. It must be pleasant news for modern science that the process of discovery is a never ending one.

How unfortunate, that still a majority of them don't believe in the Book of Allah?

45
MULTI-WORLDS AND INTELLIGENT BEINGS

A great deal of research is going on these days to discover other inhabitable worlds like the earth. A big challenge for science is to answer the question, if there are intelligent beings like the humans, anywhere else in the universe as well? Scientists are confident in the probability of there being numerous living planets like the earth all over the universe. On this subject, one is surprised to know that the Holy Qur'an starts with the existence of plurality of worlds. In its opening ayat the Qur'an says, الحمد لله رب

العالمين *"Praise worthy is Allah only Who is the Rabb (Designer, Creator and Sustainer) of the Worlds" 2(1).*

Explaining this ayat, Ibn-e-Abbas (may Allah be pleased with him) one of the companions of the Prophet (PBUH) and the earliest commentator of the Holy Qur'an had said, "There are 18,000 worlds similar to us"[25]. On this subject in ayat 65(12) the Holy Qur'an says;

$$\text{اللّٰهُ الَّذِىْ خَلَقَ سَبْعَ سَمٰوٰتٍ وَّمِنَ الْاَرْضِ مِثْلَهُنَّ ۭ يَتَنَزَّلُ الْاَمْرُ بَيْنَهُنَّ لِتَعْلَمُوْٓا اَنَّ اللّٰهَ عَلٰى كُلِّ شَىْءٍ قَدِيْرٌ ڏ وَّاَنَّ اللّٰهَ قَدْ اَحَاطَ بِكُلِّ شَىْءٍ عِلْمًا}$$

Allah is the one Who has created seven (several) heavens and (multitude of) earth like thereof. Order of Allah descends between them so that you should know that Allah is capable to do everything; And indeed Allah surrounds everything in His knowledge. [65(12)]

In ayat 45(36) the concept of plurality of worlds is mentioned separately apart from the heavens and the earth. It says,

$$\text{فَلِلّٰهِ الْحَمْدُ رَبِّ السَّمٰوٰتِ وَرَبِّ الْاَرْضِ رَبِّ الْعٰلَمِيْنَ}$$

All praises be to Allah, Sustainer and Nourisher of the heavens and the Sustainer and Nourisher of the earth, (and) Sustainer and Nourisher of the worlds. [45(36)]

---

[25] Abul-Ala-Maudoodi "Tafheem-ul-Qur'an"

Ayat 65 of sura an-Namal points out the existence of intelligent beings like us in the universe by declaring,

قُلْ لَا يَعْلَمُ مَنْ فِى السَّمٰوٰتِ وَالْاَرْضِ الْغَيْبَ اِلَّا اللّٰهُ ۚ وَمَا يَشْعُرُوْنَ اَيَّانَ يُبْعَثُوْنَ ۝

Say, Those in the heavens and the earth do not know the hidden Reality except Allah, and they don't understand when they will be raised again (for Judgement). [27(65)]

From all such ayaat of the Holy Qur'an it is quite evident that there are many more worlds in the universe that are inhabited by the intelligent being like us, and Allah is the Sustainer of all of them. In this regard modern scientific discoveries not only point out the possibility of multiple worlds like ours but to the possibilities of multiple universes also. Recent scientific thought on this subject has been summed up by Paul Davies,

> *One bold idea addresses this unnerving issue facing us is the parallel universe theory, Invented by physicist Hugh Everett in 1957, and subsequently championed by Bryce De Witt, now at the University of Texas at Austin. The theory proposes that all the possible alternative quantum worlds are equally real, and exist in parallel with one another. Whenever a measurement is performed to determine, for example, whether the cat is alive or dead, the universe divides into two, one containing a live cat, the other a dead one. Both worlds are equally real, and both contain human observers. Each set of inhabitants, however, perceives only their own branch of the universe.*

But where are these worlds? In a sense, those that closely resemble our own are very nearby. Yet they are totally inaccessible: we cannot reach them however far we travel through our own space and time. The reader of this book is no more than an inch away from millions of his duplicates, but that inch is not measured through the space of our perceptions.[26]

With this review of modern scientific thought, look again at the ayaat quoted here from the Holy Qur'an. If scientists discover intelligent beings somewhere in the universe, it will be only a confirmation of what has already been foretold by the Holy Qur'an.

How sad it is that even then most of mankind is ignorant of the Book of Allah!

46
THE END OF THE UNIVERSE

Scientists of late have accepted the fact that the universe cannot last forever. In fact, the doomsday of individual stars and galaxies is seen as a routine phenomenon. Powerful telescopes have now shown us the explosive obliteration of stars. Scientists have reason to believe that even entire galaxies, including all their content can also be annihilated and wiped off the face of the universe. Science has proved that decay of all substances to their death, is built into the design of nature. However, before 1950 the widely accepted theory about the universe was that it has always existed the way we see it now and will always continue this way. This view was challenged in 1960's and

---

[26] Davies, God,

replaced by the big bang theory. Consequently now science believes that the universe had a beginning and would have an end.

Stephen Hawking says this,

> *The universe would expand to a very large size and eventually it would collapse again into what looks like a singularity in real time.*
> *As it shrinks, heavenly bodies will lose their positions, strike with each other and explode. Ultimately, whole of the universe will shrink into a small nucleus volume. From where, it would bounce back with a huge explosion, another Big Bang.*[27]

This is similar to what has already been revealed in the Holy Qur'an. In hundreds of ayaat, it contends that the universe and everything in it, will exist only for a limited time. Eventually, like its parts, the whole universe is also destined to meet its end. Just as it had begun suddenly, so it would end suddenly too. As pointed out in the following ayaat, the end will commence with a great commotion in the heavens,

يَوْمَ تَرْجُفُ الرَّاجِفَةُ ۞ تَتْبَعُهَا الرَّادِفَةُ ۞

Think of the day, when everything will be in commotion, followed by repeated (commotions). [79(6-7)]

As mentioned in ayaat 82(1-3) this will be followed by destructive planetary collisions,

اِذَا السَّمَآءُ انْفَطَرَتْ ۞ وَاِذَا الْكَوَاكِبُ انْتَثَرَتْ ۞ وَ اِذَا الْبِحَارُ فُجِرَتْ ۞

---

[27] Stephen Hawking "A Brief History of Time", p 147

> *Think of when the heaven will be cleft asunder, planets are dispersed, and when the oceans boil over [82(1-3)]*

Near the ultimate doomsday violent disorder in the heavenly order can be visualized from ayaat 52(9-10) also,

$$\text{يَوْمَ تَمُورُ السَّمَاءُ مَوْرًا ۙ وَتَسِيرُ الْجِبَالُ سَيْرًا ۙ}$$

> *(Think of) the Day when heavens will heave with awful heaving, and the mountains (meteor) move all over. [52(9-10)]*

In this process our solar system will be destroyed. The glowing sun will lose all it brightness. As we can see from ayaat 81(1-2), it may happen in the process of large scale destruction of the galactic worlds,

$$\text{اِذَا الشَّمْسُ كُوِّرَتْ ۙ وَاِذَا النُّجُومُ انْكَدَرَتْ ۙ}$$

> *When the sun is folded up, and when the stars fall from their positions losing their lustre. [81(1-2)]*

By then however, the earth would already have been destroyed by mortal meteoric strikes,

$$\text{كَلَّا اِذَا دُكَّتِ الْاَرْضُ دَكًّا دَكًّا ۙ}$$

> *(Think of when the) Earth will be pounded to powder, ferociously (by the meteor strike) [89(21)]*

And so at dozens of places the Holy Qur'an paints out different scenarios of the impending doomsday. It also reveals that catastrophic events of doomsday will occur so suddenly that no one will be able to predict them,

يَسْـَٔلُونَكَ عَنِ السَّاعَةِ اَيَّانَ مُرْسٰىهَا ۗ قُلْ اِنَّمَا عِلْمُهَا عِنْدَ رَبِّىْ ۚ لَا يُجَلِّيْهَا لِوَقْتِهَآ اِلَّا هُوَ ۘ ثَقُلَتْ فِى السَّمٰوٰتِ وَالْاَرْضِ ۗ لَا تَأْتِيْكُمْ اِلَّا بَغْتَةً ۗ

They ask you about the Doomsday, when will it happen? Say, its knowledge is with Allah only. He alone will manifest it at its proper time. When it comes, it will be a heavy (very catastrophic) day in the heavens and earth. It will come not, but suddenly [7(187)]

47
A CONTRACTING UNIVERSE

About the question of the end of the universe, modern science now hypothesizes that it will come about after the current phase of the expansion of the universe reaches its limit, and then as a consequence of all the mass within it, the universe will start contracting. According to science, this contraction will keep increasing in velocity, as the heavenly bodies come nearer to each other and the force of gravity increases therein. Eventually planets, stars and galaxies will all start crashing against each other as the size of the universe decreases and the speed of travel of these bodies increases. However, whether the universe is presently expanding or contracting is merely conjectural. The distant galaxies that we observe today with the help of cutting edge technological equipment may only the scene that has already occurred billions of years in that past. Thus the universe may in fact already be contracting while we see it expanding.

It must surprise you that much before the discovery of science, the Holy Qur'an had already described the scene of the expansion and then the contraction of the universe, with the metaphor of the opening up of a scroll, and then it's rolling back. In this context ayat 104 of sura 21 is thought provoking,

يَوْمَ نَطْوِى السَّمَآءَ كَطَىِّ السِّجِلِّ لِلْكُتُبِ ۚ كَمَا بَدَأْنَآ أَوَّلَ خَلْقٍ نُّعِيدُهُ ۚ وَعْدًا عَلَيْنَا ۚ إِنَّا كُنَّا فَاعِلِينَ ۞

One day We shall roll up the heavens (universe) like (rolling up) a scroll of writings. Just as We did originate the first creation, We shall recreate it again. That is Our promise and We are going to do it. [21(104)]

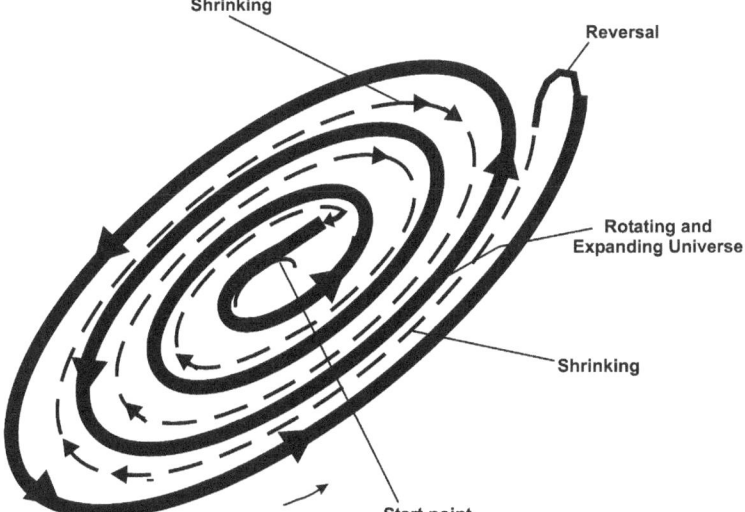

What a wonderful, comprehensive and powerful description of the origin and end of the universe! Could anyone claim knowledge of the fate of the universe with

so much certainty, in such powerful words, except the Creator Himself?

According to Hawking, the process of rolling back of the universe may take place when the inherent contracting force of gravity, possessed by the mass of all bodies within the universe overtakes the force of the initial big bang expansion. He writes in his book,

> If the density of the Universe is greater than a certain critical value, gravitational attraction will eventually stop the expansion and make the Universe start to contract again. The Universe would collapse to a big crunch. This would be rather like the big bang that began the Universe. The big crunch would be what is called a singularity, a state of infinite density at which the laws of physics would break down.[28]

With the professor's statement above in mind, now look again at the earlier quoted ayat 21(104). Was not the Holy Qur'an first to reveal the mechanism of the ultimate fate of the universe?

48
THE ROLE OF HIDDEN MATTER

How will the expansion of the universe turn into contraction? Science now believes that this will come about as a result of the enormous amount of some sort of hidden matter that is present in the Universe (or being added to it). The gravity of the mass of all this hidden matter will turn the expansion of the universe into

---

[28] Hawking, Black Holes, p 146

contraction, once the force of the initial big bang is spent and the force of gravity of the matter inside the universe takes over. About this hidden matter, Hawking says,

> *Various cosmological observations strongly suggest that there should be much more matter in our galaxy and other galaxies than we see. But one of the fundamental problems is to discover the nature of the dominant form of dark matter. Before the 1980's it was usually assumed that dark matter was ordinary matter comprised of protons, neutrons, and electrons in some not readily detectable form: perhaps gas clouds, or MACHOs — "Massive Compact Heavenly Objects" like white dwarfs or neutron stars, or even black holes.[29]*

It is truly amazing that the Holy Qur'an had already pointed out the existence of hidden matter in the universe much earlier; and that was revealed, quite significantly, in reference to the doomsday of the universe. The Qur'an calls it the 'hidden of the heavens and earth' It had revealed thus,

وَلِلَّهِ غَيْبُ السَّمٰوٰتِ وَالْأَرْضِ ۚ وَمَآ اَمْرُ السَّاعَةِ اِلَّا كَلَمْحِ الْبَصَرِ اَوْ هُوَ اَقْرَبُ ۚ اِنَّ اللّٰهَ عَلٰى كُلِّ شَيْءٍ قَدِيْرٌ ۝

And to Allah is the hidden of the heavens and the Earth, and the matter of the Doomsday, will be nothing but like a twinkling of an eye or even quicker. Surely, Allah has power over everything. [16(77)]

---

[29] Stephen Hawking, Black Holes, p 148

The first part of this revelation speaks about 'hidden of the universe' and the second part points out its relationship with the end of universe. Thus a fundamental truth is revealed here, and as is its wont, leaving the details for scientists to discover. However, one wonders, how is it that the Holy Qur'an over 1,400 years ago, had revealed the connection of hidden matter with the end of the universe, something that science could only manage to discover at the end of the twentieth century!

49
DEATH IS THE FINAL DESTINY
(THE SECOND LAW OF THERMO-DYNAMICS)

The second law of thermodynamics is a proud discovery of modern science in terms of the understanding of how nature works. It states that in every system entropy increases with time. This means that left at its own, order will automatically change into disorder unless it is checked by external intervention. Thus, if left to itself everything will decay to death. The Holy Qur'an had told the same thing as a law of nature. It reveals, **"All that exists is to perish except the Reality of your Rabb, full of Majesty and Glory." 55(26-27).** Notice here that the Holy Qur'an refers to everything that exists, and not just the living beings, in an intriguing reference to the destruction of the every thing in the universe at their turn.

Ayat 28(88) also mentions the same fact in slightly different terms,

كُلُّ شَيْءٍ هَالِكٌ اِلَّا وَجْهَهُ ۚ لَهُ الْحُكْمُ وَاِلَيْهِ تُرْجَعُوْنَ

Everything is to perish except the Reality of your Lord. To Him is to rule and to Him is the final return.

This is the universal principle. The process of death is part of life. In scientific terminology it means that entropy is bound to rise in every thing. The only exception is the Supreme Creator Himself. According to this principle, nothing can survive forever, even the highly stable particles like protons must decay with time, and ultimately perish.

At the cosmic level, the Holy Qur'an revealed that the sun and all the stars will die in their time arrives. For example ayat 81(1-2) has categorically stated,

اِذَا الشَّمْسُ كُوِّرَتْ ۞ وَاِذَا النُّجُوْمُ انْكَدَرَتْ ۞

(Think of the Time) when the sun will cease to shine, and when the stars will lose their lustre [81(1-2)]

According to modern science the sun has already reached its middle age in terms of its life span. It is estimated that in other 5-6 billion years it will exhaust all its fuel and turn into a black dwarf. However, accidents of nature can hasten the process of its death. On this subject Davies writes in his book,

> *As far as the sun is concerned, it clearly cannot continue burning away merrily ad infinitum. Year by year its fuel reserves decline, so that eventually it will cool and dim. By the same token its fires must have*

been ignited only a finite time ago: it does not have unlimited sources of energy.³⁰

As for the existence of the universe Davies sums up today's scientific thought,

> *If the universe has a finite stock of order, and is changing irreversibly towards disorder - ultimately to thermodynamic equilibrium - two very deep inferences follow immediately. The first is that the universe will eventually die, wallowing, as the 'heat death' of the universe. The second is that the universe cannot have existed forever; otherwise it would have reached its equilibrium end state an infinite time ago. Conclusion: The Universe did not always exist and likewise is not eternal either.*³¹

This is the same conclusion what could be derived from the general principle revealed in the Holy Qur'an over fourteen hundred years ago, **"Everything will Perish eventually" 28(88)** كُلُّ شَيْءٍ هَالِكٌ. It should certainly surprise every rational mind that how could someone in those days of 'Ignorance', more than 1400 years ago narrate such facts about nature so precisely and with so much certainty. The only valid explanation is that the Holy Qur'an is a revelation from the Creator of the Universe, and Muhammad (PBUH) is His messenger. How unfortunate it is that most people still do not have faith in this!

---

30   Davies, God
31   Davies, God

50
SPACE TRAVEL AND SPACE HAZARDS

Space travel is amongst the greatest testimonials to mankind's scientific advancement. Technological development in rocket sciences resulted in the landing of man on the moon in 1969. Since then much more powerful rockets have been developed for even deeper space travel, and to establish space stations. Moreover, thousands of communication satellites are encircling the earth at all times. Unmanned space vehicles have been sent for deep space exploration. It seems entirely possible that man may colonize its near space regions before the turn of the century.

It is stunning thus, to see that the Holy Qur'an had already prophesied about this achievement more than fourteen centuries ago. It was revealed then that man will one day leave the boundaries of earth, once he acquires sufficient power. Thus achievement has been termed as great favour if Allah to man. In this context, ayat 33-34 of sura Ar-Rahman are incredibly thought provoking,

يَمَعْشَرَ الْجِنِّ وَالْإِنْسِ اِنِ اسْتَطَعْتُمْ اَنْ تَنْفُذُوْا مِنْ اَقْطَارِ السَّمٰوٰتِ وَالْاَرْضِ فَانْفُذُوْا ۚ لَاتَنْفُذُوْنَ اِلَّا بِسُلْطٰنٍ ۚ فَبِاَىِّ اٰلَآءِ رَبِّكُمَا تُكَذِّبٰنِ ۚ

O you assembly of Jinns and Men! If it be, you can pass beyond the boundaries of the heavens and the earth, pass ye! You will not be able to pass through without acquiring great power. Then which of the favours of your Rabb will you deny.
[55(33-34)]

It is worth contemplating the idea of 'boundaries of the heavens and the earth', mentioned in this ayat. This refers to the region of neutral gravity. A rocket needs initial velocity to break through earth's gravitational barrier at the speed of around 19 miles/second. After this, the rocket could continue travelling effortlessly.

It is no less surprising that the Holy Qur'an had also pointed out the perils of space travel. In the following ayat 55(35) it mentions that during space journeys, man would encounter violent radiation storms. It says,

يُرْسَلُ عَلَيْكُمَا شُوَاظٌ مِّنْ نَّارٍ ۙ وَّنُحَاسٌ فَلَا تَنتَصِرَانِ ۞

(As you travel in space) On you will be sent flares of smokeless fire and burning hot flames, so then no defence will ye have against them. *[55(35)]*

Latest scientific finds confirm the possible dangers of cosmic radiation in outer space. It has been discovered that outer space is under constant bombardment by different types of cosmic radiations from all sides. For example, hot plasma flares keep storming out from the sun continuously, which can damage space vehicles, as well as satellites in their way. In view of such dangers, NASA has started monitoring solar weather for the safety of space vehicles on a continuous basis.

Doubtless these are great scientific achievements, but it is no less astounding, that the Holy Qur'an had foretold space travels and its impending dangers, more than 1,400 years ago. Could anyone else had thought of it then? Have you any explanation of it?

Will you still not believe in Muhammad (PBUH) and the revelation bestowed upon him from on high?

51
THE ABSOLUTENESS OF SCIENTIFIC LAWS AND PROGRAMMED NATURE

One of the fundamental discoveries of modern science is that nature abides by certain laws, all over the space-time continuum. This principle is the basic premise of Einstein's theory of relativity. It might therefore, surprise you that it was the Holy Qur'an that first revealed this truth of nature as well. It is pointed out in ayat 10(64) that commandments of Allah *Subhana-Hu* never change.

لَا تَبْدِيلَ لِكَلِمٰتِ اللَّهِ ۚ

There is absolutely no change in the commandments of Allah [10(64)]

In ayat 30 of sura ar-Roum it is revealed,

لَا تَبْدِيلَ لِخَلْقِ اللَّهِ ۚ ذَٰلِكَ الدِّينُ الْقَيِّمُ ۙ

There will be no change in the creative ways of Allah. That is the fixed system [30(30)]

And in ayat 46(3) it is further stated,

مَاخَلَقْنَا السَّمٰوٰتِ وَالْاَرْضَ وَمَابَيْنَهُمَآ اِلَّا بِالْحَقِّ وَاَجَلٍ مُّسَمًّى ۚ

We have not created the heavens and the earth and all that lies between them but with a definite purpose; and for an appointed term only [46(3)]

As for the programmed nature, it is revealed,

سَبِّحِ اسْمَ رَبِّكَ الْأَعْلَى ۝ الَّذِى خَلَقَ فَسَوَّى ۝ وَالَّذِى قَدَّرَ فَهَدَى ۝

Glorify the Name of your Lord Who created, then arranged them in definite proportions and then measured them precisely, thereby gave them their Nature. [87(1-3)]

It also presented the general rule,

لِكُلِّ نَبَإٍ مُّسْتَقَرٌّ ۚ وَسَوْفَ تَعْلَمُونَ ۝

For every event (order) is a program and in due course of time you shall come to know of it [6(67)]

All this means that nature is geared to abide by the laws of Allah, and that these natural laws do not change with time and space. Universe is a pre-programmed system to last for an appointed term. Indeed, the permanence of natural laws is the basic assumption in scientific research and analysis. On this Hawking says in his book *"The fundamental postulate of Theory of Relativity, as it was called, was that the laws of science should be the same for all freely moving observers, no matter what their speed"*[32].

In the same context Einstein is reported to have said, *"Those individuals to whom we owe the great creative achievements of science were all of them filled with truly religious conviction that this Universe of ours is something perfect"*[33].

---

[32] Stephen Hawking "A Brief History of Time", p 21, Bantam Books, 1996
[33] Ken Wilber, "Quantum Questions" Shambhala, p 113

As you can see in ayat 6(67) above, the Holy Qur'an had also predicted that before long, man will discover the facts revealed in the Holy Qur'an by himself. Now everyone believes in the universal transcendence of scientific laws. This way modern science has in fact emerged as a strong witness to the truth of the Holy Qur'an.

Indeed when the Qur'an was being revealed, no human could conceive of these facts of nature. Man's knowledge was extremely limited then and all that he knew or cared about was restricted to his immediate environment. The assertion about the pre-programmed quality of the universe and the permanence of the laws of nature, could not possibly have been the handiwork of any man. Alas, even then a majority of people do not believe!

52
QUANTUM CREATIONS

Does nature operate in a continuous, gradual, evolutionary fashion, or in sudden creative jumps? This has been a major question for scientists since Newton's time. Up-till the beginning of the twentieth century, the idea of slow acting evolutionary development was, sort of accepted theory. But things changed by 1930 due to the new discoveries about the sub-atomic particles.

Finally Quantum Mechanics took birth, after the discovery that electrons travel from one orbit to other in jumps and in fixed quanta. Earlier it was thought that motion is continuous, like that of waves on the mysterious media called ether. Quantum mechanics rejected the idea of ether and the continuous movement of particle and instead proposed that at least at the atomic level, events do occur in quantum, jumps of discrete measure. For example, light is composed of particles called photons which hop over in space while travelling.

One is surprised that, the 'rules of creation' given in the Holy Qur'an also point out to the discrete, quantum characteristic of things. It speaks of the creative mode of Allah *Subhana-Hu* according to the principle of *'Kun Faya-Koon'* (كن فيكون) ie "'Be', and it is there". In this respect ayat 82 of sura Yasin declares,

اِنَّمَآ اَمرُهٗ اِذَا اَرَادَ شَيْئًا اَنْ يَّقُوْلَ لَهٗ كُنْ فَيَكُوْنُ ۞

Surely His Command, when He intends a thing is simply that He would say to it "Be" and it is there. [36(82)]

Allah being the Supreme Creator, it should be evident from such ayaat of the Holy Qur'an that creative strokes will always take place in pre-programmed discrete measure. However, the Holy Qur'an also supports slow evolutionary development process. Thus the overall process of creation and development will consist of sudden creative quantum activity, and further development in the slow evolutionary manner as shown in the figure above. Thus according to the Holy Qur'an both the Newtonian mechanics as well as quantum mechanics have their role in nature.

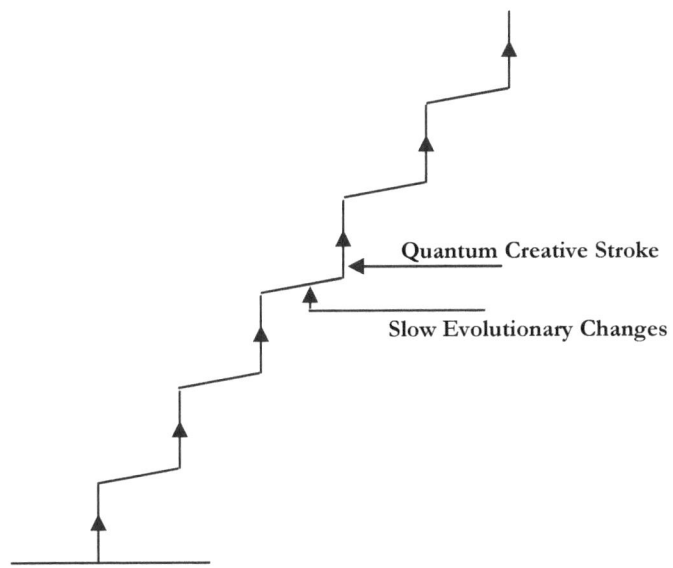

Fig: Creative activity in quantum jumps, and slow evolutionary development, both are part of nature

53
THE ATMOSPHERIC ROOF

Amongst the significant discoveries of the twentieth century was that the earth is enveloped by layers of atmosphere which serve the vital function of protecting life on earth from cosmic radiations as well as from meteor strikes, both of which keep relentlessly bombarding the earth. These atmospheric barriers act as a roof over us and thus keep us safely ensconced within. Meteors are either destroyed or reduced to insignificant rubble before reaching the earth. This happens due to the insurmountable friction that the atmospheric air cover offers to these stray meteors. Indeed without this protective roof, life could not possibly have survived on earth.

Lately, substantial research has been conducted on this subject, and which shows that the atmosphere is divided into seven layers, one above the other. It might shock you again to know that many centuries prior to this scientific discovery, the Holy Qur'an had revealed that there is an atmospheric roof over the earth that consists of seven strong barriers, layer upon layer. Here is the original Qur'anic revelation,

وَلَقَدْ خَلَقْنَا فَوْقَكُمْ سَبْعَ طَرَآئِقَ وَمَا كُنَّا عَنِ الْخَلْقِ غَافِلِينَ

Indeed We created above you seven layers (ways) and We are not unmindful (to the safety of) Our creatures [23(17)]

Note the reason given in the ayat above for the seven layer atmospheric system: it is for the safety of the creations of Allah *Subhana-Hu* on earth. Ayat 78(12), points out that these seven atmospheric systems are very strong. وَبَنَيْنَا فَوْقَكُمْ سَبْعًا شِدَادًا **"And We have built above you seven very strong (systems)"** 78(12).

The Holy Qur'an points out the facts of nature, leaving details for the man to discover and analyse, just as a great architect would provide a general outline for his apprentices to subsequently fill in. The atmospheric roof over the earth has now been found to be composed of the following seven spheres:

1. Tropo-sphere – in it cloud formation takes place, changes in weather also occurs in it. It is about 18 km high;
2. Strato-sphere – up to 51 km high. Uppermost part of it consists of the ozone layer, which absorbs the harmful ultraviolet radiation emitted by the sun;
3. Meso-sphere – up to 85 km high. In this sphere temperature may fall to -73°C, and provides a cooling effect to the earth;
4. Thermo-sphere – up to 500 km high. Temperatures here rise to between 50 °C and 120°C. It absorbs cosmic radiation;
5. Iono-sphere – this is above 500 km. It reflects radio waves, thereby allowing long distance communication. It also reflects certain dangerous cosmic radiation back to space;
6. Exo-sphere – this stretches over 1,000 km. It slows down falling meteors directed to the earth; and
7. Magneto-sphere – it is between 3,000 to 30,000 km high. It reflects high energy particles away from earth. Van Allan radiation belt also lies in it.

One wonders in amazement how the Holy Qur'an could inform us about the astonishing system of atmospheric roof consisting of seven protective layers above the earth for the safety of life on it at a time when nobody had any idea of such things. Could it be the work of a genius, or the revelation from the Creator of the universes? Alas! Most of the mankind still do not heed to the Holy Qur'an for guidance in their life.

54
PROTECTION OF THE ENVIRONMENT

Global environment has turned into one of the most significant and hotly debated issues in the world. In view of the potentially fatal consequences of environmental pollution, it has become one of the most serious problems faced by mankind. Various UN environmental conferences have stressed the issue and have warned that if immediate protective measures are not taken now, then the ultimate survival of life on earth will be threatened. If the present dangerous trends continue, then in near future, the problem may turn into an irretrievable catastrophe.

According to C. R. Kitchin,

> *Great concern is currently being felt over the 'greenhouse effect', the slow increase in the amount of carbon dioxide in the Earth's atmosphere due to the consumption of fossil fuels and reduction in plant biomass, leading to increases in the average surface temperature of the Earth. The effect is exacerbated by consequent increased release of methane and the evaporation of water as the temperature rises, because all these gases allow through the short-wave radiations from the Sun whilst trapping the long-wave radiations back into space by the Earth. Dire predictions of rise in the global average temperature by the middle of the next century are given.*
>
> *The effects of such an increase, even though of only a few degrees, may well be drastic. Sea levels may rise to wipe out low-lying countries like Bangladesh and the Netherlands and put many cities and ports in*

danger. The level will rise not because of the often-mentioned melting of the polar caps, but because the sea water will expand in volume as its temperature rises. Climatic patterns will also shift, and agricultural zones will change.

That in turn would raise the temperature further, releasing yet more gases and so on, a positive feedback loop with disastrous consequences for most life on Earth. The final surface temperatures might possibly exceed the boiling point of water.[34]

How thoughtless of man that besides degradation of physical environment he has also polluted his social and spiritual values a great deal, resulting in unwanted tensions, mental disorders, broken homes and psychic problems. Responsibility for this rests to a large extent upon the rich, industrially developed nations due to the wastes and pollutants produced by their wasteful industrial economies and commercial moral standards. However, under threat of the rising levels of pollutions, "Save the Environment" is now the biggest concern of the United Nations as well.

Could the Creator of the worlds have remained silent on this issue of such great magnitude in His revelations to mankind? Indeed, He had very strongly warned mankind not to give way to spoiling the equilibrium established on earth by Him. Man was advised thus,

---

[34] C.R. Kitchen "Journey to the End of Universe", Adam Hilger, USA, 1990

وَلَا تُفْسِدُوا فِى الْأَرْضِ بَعْدَ إِصْلَاحِهَا ذَٰلِكُمْ خَيْرٌ لَّكُمْ إِن كُنتُم مُّؤْمِنِينَ ۚ

Do not spoil the equilibrium on the earth, after it has been stabilized. This is better for you, if you believe. [7(85)]

Similar warnings are given in sura al-Baqara, ayat 11, and sura al-Araaf, ayat 56.
Here is a great lesson for the modern man. Even if he is not a Muslim, he must heed the advice of the Holy Qur'an about global environment. We must not disturb the sensitive equilibrium and balance of the earth's environment and regenerative mechanisms.

At the same time one asks in wonder, how could someone over 1,400 years ago have thought of warning mankind about the dangers of disturbing the equilibrium of earth? Was he a great scientist or the inspired messenger of Allah? How unfortunate, even then that many don't believe in him!

55
WATER, THE SOURCE OF LIFE

Where did life begin initially? This has been a mind boggling question for science until recently. It was only in the mid twentieth century that science could say with confidence that life first evolved in water and that water is essential for its survival. In this regard Carl Sagan writes in his book[35],

---

[35] Carl Sagan "Cosmos", p 44, Abacus, reprinted 1998

We know from the fossil records that the origin of life happened soon after, perhaps around 4 billion years ago, in the ponds and oceans of the primitive Earth. The first living things were not anything so complex as a one-celled organism, already a highly sophisticated form of life. The first stirrings were much more humble. In those early days, lightning and ultraviolet light from the Sun were breaking apart the simple hydrogen-rich molecules of the primitive atmosphere, the fragments spontaneously recombining into more and more complex molecules. The products of this early chemistry were dissolved in the oceans, forming a kind of organic soup of gradually increasing complexity, until one day, quite by accident, a molecule arose that was able to make crude copies of itself, using as building blocks other molecules in the soup.

Discovery about the origin of life in water is no doubt a matter of pride for science. But it might surprise the scientific community that the Holy Qur'an had revealed this truth much earlier. It revealed that life began in murky pools of water and for its survival, depends on water.

In very plain words it declares:-

"All things living We made from water. Will they even then not believe?" (sura al-Ambia, ayat 30.)

It means that water is the fundamental source of every bind of life. If there is no water there will be no life also.

Today search for living beings in outer space is based on the assumption, that the presence of water would identify the pre-requisite for life. The crucial second part of the revelation quoted above, is an important piece of advice for the non-believers, *"Will they even then not believe?"*

Let the non-believers ponder over this revelation in all honesty. How could someone over 1,400 years ago, make this scientific assertion in such clear terms about the riddle of life's origin, if he was not inspired by the Creator of life Himself? Alas! Even then they do not believe in him!

56
THE INVISIBLE BARRIER BETWEEN WATER STREAMS

Scientific research in recent years has seen two contrasting streams of water in the oceans, with divergent properties, flowing side by side, with an invisible barrier between them. This barrier divides bodies of water so that each stream independently flowing in the sea has its own temperature, salinity and density. Long before its discovery by scientific research, the Holy Qur'an had already pointed out the phenomena of the existence of such distinctive streams of water.

Ayaat 55(19-20) of sura Ar-Rahman point out that it is a blessing of Allah *Subhana-Hu* that there are two bodies of water in the oceans flowing side by side, yet not mixing together He has created a barrier between them,

مَرَجَ الْبَحْرَيْنِ يَلْتَقِيَانِ ۞ بَيْنَهُمَا بَرْزَخٌ لَّا يَبْغِيَانِ ۞ فَبِأَيِّ آلَاءِ رَبِّكُمَا تُكَذِّبَانِ ۞

He has let free two ocean streams flowing side by side each other. In between them is an unseen barrier. They do not take over each other. Then which of the favour of your Rabb will you deny [55(19-21)]

According to I. A. Ibrahim[36], "One example of these rivers in the ocean is the Gulf Stream, beginning in the Caribbean and ending in the North Atlantic. This extensive western boundary current plays an important role in the pole-ward transfer of heat and salt, and serves to warm the European continent. It begins upstream of Cape Hatteras, where the Florida Current ceases to follow the continental shelf. The position of the stream as it leaves the coast changes throughout the year. In the fall, it shifts north, while in the winter and early spring it shifts south.[37]

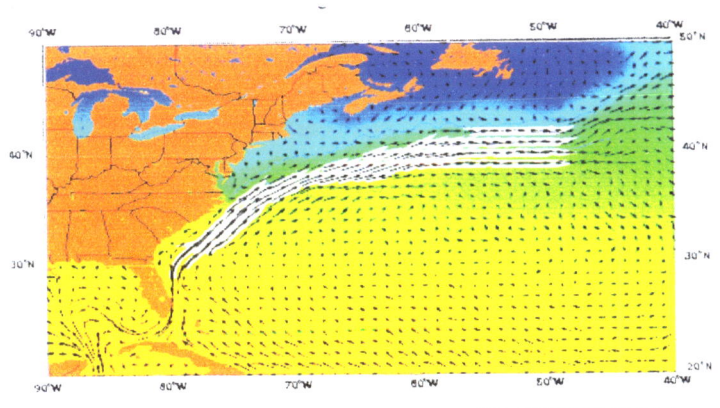

Fig: The Gulf Stream as represented by the Mariano Global Surface Velocity Analysis (MGSVA).

---

[36] I. A. Ibrahim, "A Brief Guide to Understanding of Islam", Darussalam, Houston
[37] Auer, 1987, Kelly and Gille, 1990, Frankignoul et al, 2001

Compared to the width of the current, which is 100-200 km, the range of its variation, 30-40 km, is relatively small (Hogg and Johns 1995). When the Mediterranean sea water enters the Atlantic over the Gibraltar sill, it moves several hundred kilometres into the Atlantic at a depth of about 1,000 meters with its own warm, saline, and less dense characteristics. The Mediterranean water stabilizes at this depth".

Just imagine, how any man could possibly have spoken of hydro barriers in oceans so precisely and comprehensively, during what is known as the Dark Age? Still some people, out of their prejudice, doubt the Holy Qur'an as a revelation from the Creator of the worlds.

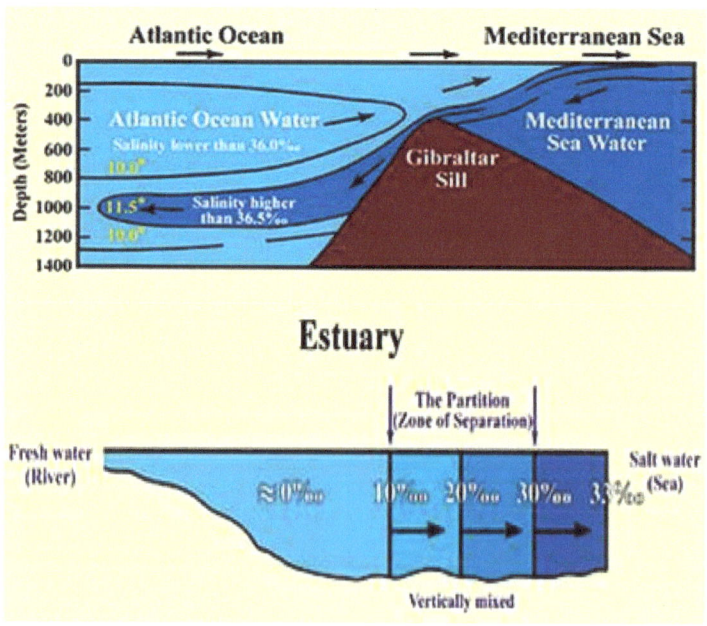

Fig: Parallel streams of water in oceans

57
EXISTENCE IN PAIRS

One of the greatest discoveries of twentieth century physics was the Noble Prize winning work of Paul Dirac that concerned matter and anti-matter. Dirac discovered in 1933 that the universe was created out of nothing into positive and negative pairs of matter and anti-matter. According to Prof Abdus Salam, *"He could show in general grounds that all particles in nature must exist in pairs; that to every particle there must correspond an anti-particles of precisely the same mass: the same spin but of opposite electrical charge"*[38]. From this, one could infer the possibility of the existence of the pairs of universe and anti-universe as well. Later, when the truth of this hypothesis was verified experimentally, Dirac duly received his Noble Prize.

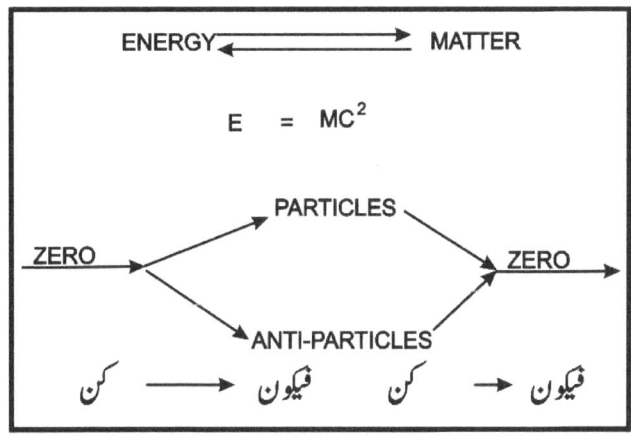

---

[38] Prof. Abdus Salam "Symmetry Concepts in Modern Physics", PAEC, Lahore, 1966

In its generalized form, the hypothesis that all particles in the universe exist in pairs, is now seen as a fundamental law of nature.

Long before its discovery by modern science, the Holy Qur'an had already intimated the fact of all creation by Allah in pairs, whether known or unknown to man. So matter and anti-matter, everything without exception must exist in the form of pairs. The following revelation of sura Al-Zaariat ayat 49 states this fact,

ومن كل شئ خلقنا زوجين لعلكم تزكرون

"We have created pairs in everything, May be you reflect into it to learn some lesson" 51(49).

Ayat 36 of sura Yasin informs us that there is no exception to this rule. All the known and the unknown things follow this low. It says,

سُبْحٰنَ الَّذِيْ خَلَقَ الْاَزْوَاجَ كُلَّهَا مِمَّا تُنْبِتُ الْاَرْضُ وَمِنْ اَنْفُسِهِمْ وَمِمَّا لَا يَعْلَمُوْنَ ۞

All praise for He (Allah) Who has created everything in pairs, those which grow in the Earth, And in your own selves, and those which you do not know (yet) [36(36)]

As already stated earlier in this book, science has in fact turned out to be a supporter of the revelations of the Holy Qur'an. By its discovery, science has confirmed the truth revealed in the Qur'an that all existence occurs in pairs throughout nature. For instance, every action has a reaction; electromagnetism exists in a pair of magnetic and electrical fields. A positive charge always induces a corresponding negative charge. Magnetic polarity also goes in pairs. Atomic structure down to its sub-atomic level follows the same principle. Matter and energy form another pair, expressed by the equation $e = mc^2$. In the biological world too, the same truth is seen at every level. For example blood consists of red and white cells, and it comprises of x- and y-chromosomes. Everyone has a pair of eyes, pair of ears and pair of left- and right-side of the brain, and so on.

According to this revelation, discovery of one thing naturally points to the presence of its pair. On the much larger scale, this also leads to the possibility of existence of parallel universes which is now a serious subject for scientific research. Scientists claim having discovered the twin of our own sun as well. Thus with time, the Qur'anic rule of creation in pairs is emerging as the basic scientific truth about all levels of nature. Think about it, could anyone possibly have pronounced this fundamental reality, so comprehensively over 1,400 years ago, unless he was inspired directly by the Creator Himself? Will you then still not believe that the Holy Qur'an is the revelation from Allah *Subhana-Hu?*

58
ROOTS OF MOUNTAINS

Modern earth sciences have proven that mountains have deep roots under the surface of the ground. These roots may be several times deeper than the heights of the mountains. So they are like the pegs that go right down to the crust of the earth. Scientifically, the concept of mountains as pegs and having roots in the ground was introduced only in the latter half of the nineteenth century.

Before that scientific knowledge about them was non-existent.

It is therefore quite surprising that the metaphor used for mountains in the Holy Qur'an is also pegs in the ground, as we see it in the following ayaat,

اَلَمْ نَجْعَلِ الْاَرْضَ مِهٰدًا ۞ وَّالْجِبَالَ اَوْتَادًا ۞

Have We not made the earth a wide soft expanse, and the mountains like pegs? [78(6-7)]

According to I. A. Ibrahim, Professor Emeritus Frank Press who was the Science Advisor to former US President Jimmy Carter, and who has also been the President of the National Academy of Sciences, Washington, in his book "Earth" writes that mountains have underlying roots. These roots are deeply embedded in the ground. Therefore, mountains have a shape like the pegs as you can see in figure below,[39]

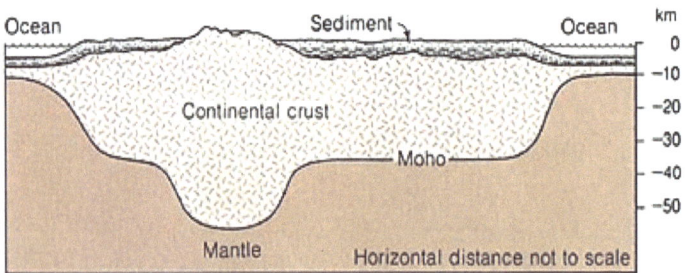

Fig: Mountains have deep roots under the surface (Press and Siever *"Earth"* p 413)

---

[39] I. A. Ibrahim "A Brief Guide to Understanding Islam", Darussalam, Houston

Besides the fact that mountains are like pegs in the floor of the earth, the Holy Qur'an also mentioned the astounding fact that they help stabilize the earth. It says at 16(15), *"And He has set firm mountains in the earth so that it would not shake with you."* The role of mountains as stabilizers of the earth has just recently begun to be understood in the framework of plate tectonics. One wonders how could the Holy Qur'an have presented such scientific facts fourteen centuries ago if it was not itself the handiwork of the Creator of the worlds!

59
THE Qur'an ON HUMAN EMBRYONIC DEVELOPMENT

Information given in several ayaat of the Holy Qur'an about human embryonic development is extremely revealing in light of the latest scientific discoveries. One wonders how Muhammad (PBUH) could possibly have known all that is presented in the Holy Qur'an so accurately over 1,400 years ago. For example, look at the following revelations,

> *We created man from an extract of clay, then We kept him as a tiny drop in a place of settlement, firmly fixed. Then We made this tiny drop into an Alaqah (process of joining one thing with other), then We made the Alaqah into a Mughdah (chewed gum-like substance) [23(12-14)]*

This revelation has two parts: first, human origin in the marshy pool of clay wherefrom, a single cell begins its life which gradually evolves to produce the body of man. The second part is about creation by the normal reproduction process. In this process childbirth passes through three stages, expressed by the words 'nutfa' (نطفه), 'alaqah' (علقه) and 'mughdah'. Nutfa is a tiny drop of the emission of the father, which travels through the vaginal path to fertilize the mother's ovum. Alaqah is the process of joining male sperm (nutfa) with the egg of the mother. Then starts a rapid reaction of cell multiplication in which the embryo is formed, which is of the shape of 'mughdah'. The Arabic word mudghah means 'chewed gum-like substance'. If one were to take a piece of gum and chew it in his mouth, and then compare it with the embryo at the mudghah stage, the similarity between the appearances of the two would become obvious. This is because of the somites at the back of the embryo.

The word 'alaqah' is also taken to mean blood clot. The external appearance of the embryo during the alaqah stage is similar to that of a blood clot. This is due to the presence of relatively large amount of blood in the embryo during this stage. Also during this stage, blood in the embryo does not circulate, until the end of the third week. Thus the embryo at this stage looks like a clot of blood.

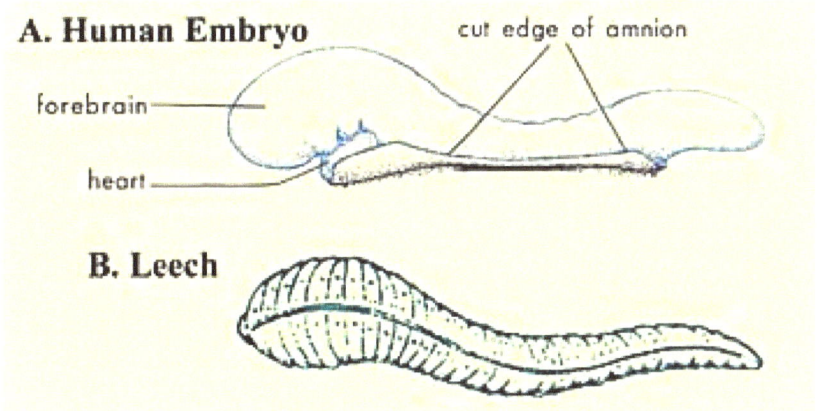

Fig: Drawings illustrating the similarities in appearance between a leech and a human embryo in the Mughdian stage (embryo drawing from the "Developing Human", Moore and Persaud, 5th ed, p 73)

Professor Keith Moore who is one of the world's leading authorities in the fields of anatomy and embryology said this during the Seventh Medical Conference in Dammam, Saudi Arabia in 1981, As far as it is known from the history of embryology, little was known about the staging and classification of human embryos until the twentieth century. For this reason, the descriptions of the human embryo in the Qur'an cannot be based on scientific knowledge in the seventh century. The only reasonable conclusion is that these descriptions were revealed to Muhammad (PBUH) from God. (36).

During one discussion forum, Professor Moore stated,

"It has been a great pleasure for me to help clarify statements in the Qur'an about human development. It

is clear to me that these statements must have come to Muhammad (PBUH) from God, because almost all of this knowledge was not discovered until many centuries later. This proves to me that Muhammad (PBUH) must have been a messenger of God." (36)

In the course of this discussion, Professor Moore was asked the obvious question, "does this mean that you believe that the Qur'an is the Word of God?" He replied, "I find no difficulty in accepting this". Will you also accept this?

60
JUST PONDER

In this part of the book we have looked at some of the greatest discoveries of modern science, and compared them to the revelations of the Holy Qur'an over 1,400 years ago. From this comparison we have to agree that either Muhammad (PBUH) was the greatest scientist of all times, and of course he must also have had a team of experts and owned well-equipped laboratories; if not, then we must acknowledge that he must have been directly inspired by the Creator of the worlds.

Thus the Holy Qur'an is a challenge to every living soul. How is it that someone who had never attended school – in fact who lived amongst the least educated people on earth – could reveal so many fundamental truths about nature in concise terms, in the seventh century? It is an absolute impossibility, except of course if he was the true messenger of Allah. He was sent to the world to guide mankind towards highest spiritual and physical achievements. The Holy Qur'an is his eternal miracle.

Indeed, where science ends, Qur'an begins. The Holy Qur'an is not a book of science, but a book about the basic truths of physical as well as metaphysical worlds. Details of the socio-spiritual life were left to the messenger of Allah to demonstrate with his personal example. Scientific and technical details were left for the people who came after him to explore.

In light of all this, there can be no any excuse to disbelieve in the Holy Qur'an.

Your success in this world and salvation in the life Hereafter lies in the whole hearted acknowledgement of the fact that, acceptance of this truth and then follow it in letter and spirit to mould your lives accordingly. It begin with the,

There is no God but Allah and Muhammad is the Messenger of Allah
لا اله الا الله محمد الرسول الله

Part III

The Irrefutable Mathematical Miracles of The Holy Qur'an

61
MATHEMATICAL MIRACLES OF THE HOLY Qur'an

Mathematics is the exact science. It provides the final proof of the truth of a scientific theory. The Holy Qur'an also offers itself to this test. In the following pages we shall place before the readers some of the mind boggling mathematical miracles of the Holy Qur'an as the irrefutable proofs that it is the Book from the Creator of the worlds. Alas! Many of us do not find time for it.

62
THE RELATIONSHIP BETWEEN THE SOLAR AND THE LUNAR YEARS

Scientific knowledge about the exact relation between solar and lunar years is quite recent. Not very long ago a solar year was considered to be of 365 days and lunar year of 354 days duration. By the end of the twentieth century, with the accuracy achieved in measuring time, the precise measurement of a solar year has been determined as 365.2422 days ie 365 days, 5 hours, 48 minutes and 46.08 seconds and the lunar year as equal to 354.60394 days ie 354 days, 14 hours, 29 minutes and 24 seconds.

The ratio of a lunar year to a solar year is 354.60394 divided by 365.2422, which is 0.970073.

Let us turn to the Holy Qur'an. More than fourteen hundred years ago, while narrating the history of the people of the Cave in sura al-Kahaf ayat 25, it pointed out that 300 solar years are equal to 309 lunar years.

وَلَبِثُوا فِي كَهْفِهِمْ ثَلَاثَ مِائَةٍ سِنِينَ وَازْدَادُوا تِسْعًا ۞ قُلِ اللَّهُ أَعْلَمُ بِمَا لَبِثُوا ۖ لَهُ غَيْبُ السَّمَاوَاتِ وَالْأَرْضِ ۖ

*And they stayed in their cave three hundred years (solar calendar), and add nine to it (for lunar calendar) say, Allah knows the best how long did they stay there. To Him is the (knowledge) of all the hidden in the heaven and earth.
[18(25-26)]*

Here is a test of the truth of the Qur'an. If it is from Allah, then 300 solar years must be exactly equal to 309 lunar years.

Let us verify this by calculating the ratio been 300 and 309. If the Qur'an is right it should be the same as 0.970073, as per the latest scientific data about solar and lunar years...

$$300/309 = 0.970073!!$$

We can cross verify it by calculating the number of days in 300 solar years and those in 309 lunar years. They must be equal.

Days in 300 solar years: 300x365.2422   =
109,572.66 days
Days in 309 lunar years: 309x354.6039   =
109,572.66 days

How wonderful, it is exactly the same as calculated above using the latest measurements of the length of the solar and lunar years by science. One wonders how could Muhammad (Peace be upon him) have known that 300 solar years were exactly equal to 309 lunar years a fact which even science could not dare say only few years ago! There can be no other explanation but that he was the true prophet of Allah, inspired from the creator of the worlds, and the Holy Qur'an is the revelation from Him.

63
THE RELATIONSHIP BETWEEN OCEANS AND THE DRY LAND ON EARTH IN THE QUR'AN

Usually the ratio of oceans to dry land on the surface of the earth is said to be 75/25. That is, the oceans are said to cover 75% of the face of the earth. However, we know now after the development of satellite imagery that this rule of thumb figure is not precisely accurate. In reality, it has been discovered that dry land is precisely 28.8888% and the remaining 71.1111% area is under water.
Let us now turn to the Holy Qur'an.

In the entire Qur'an the word 'barr' (بر) which means 'dry land' is used 13 times, whereas the word 'bahar' (بحر) which means 'ocean', including rivers, and lakes occurs 32 times (total 13 + 32 = 45).

Here is a remarkable relationship between land and under water areas on earth. Accordingly, on a percentage basis dry land ratio to the total surface of the earth will be 13 divided by 45 ie
$$13 / 45 \times 100 = 28.8888\%$$

And the percentage of oceans will be
$$32 / 45 \times 100 = 71.1111\%$$

One is wonderstruck by this exact match with the latest discoveries of science. If anyone thinks that Muhammad (Peace be upon him) was the author of the Qur'an, then two things are obvious: one, that he was intimately aware of the earth's geography, and second, that he had counted the occurrence of the words barr (بر) and bahar (بحر) in his book and then adjusted them to match the numbers required for the precise ratio between the dry and watery areas on earth. Could he have performed such an incredible scientific wonder 1,400 years ago? If not, then you should get rid of your prejudices and acknowledge that the Holy Qur'an must be the revelation from Allah, the Creator of the worlds, and that Muhammad (Peace be upon him) is the true messenger of Allah.

64
THE MIRACULOUS MATHEMATICAL BASIS OF THE HOLY QUR'AN

Research conducted in the structure and arrangement of the Holy Qur'an into words, ayaat and suras reveal an extraordinary mathematical marvel. Its letters, words, sentences and chapters are designed and arranged according to a very special mathematical code. In this design, the number 19 holds the key position[40].

This number is typical in mathematics also. It is non-divisible by any number, is made of the first and the last integer of Arabic numerals, and if you add (9+1) it converges to 10 which converge to Unity (1+0=1). In the

---

[40] Rashid Khalifa, "The Qur'an, the Visual Presentation of a Miracle, Islamic Production, Arizone U.S.A. 1989

holy Qur'an this number occurs only once in Ayat 30 of sura Al-Muddaththir where it is revealed that there are 19 guards on Hell fire. Thus the number "19" may have something to do with the Qur'anic security system also. If one attempts to change anything in the Holy Qur'an then this code will give the alarm bell.

When researchers started counting with the help of computers, the words and letters in the text of the Holy Qur'an they were surprised to note that the occurrence of many of the words and letters was a multiple of 19. Initially the researchers took it to be mere coincidence. But it was clearly more than a coincidence, as they fathomed the pervasive nature of the phenomenon throughout the Qur'an.

This miracle starts with the very first ayat (بسم الله الرحمن الرحيم) of the Holy Qur'an, which consists of four words, Ism, Allah, Ar-Rahman and Ar-Raheem; in all comprising of 19 letters.

م ى ح ر ل ا ن م ح ر ل ا ه ل ل ا م س ب
19 18 17 16 15 14 13 12 11 10 9 8 7 6 5 4 3 2 1

The constituent words of this ayat i.e. Ism (اسم) Allah (الله), Rehmaan (رحمن) and Raheem (رحيم) constituting بسم الله الرحمن الرحيم)) are counted as 19, 2099, 57, 114 times, respectively, in the main text of the Holy Qur'an. Each of this number is the straight multiple of 19 with the exception of the word Allah that occurs 2099 times i.e. 142x19+1. It should be like this because name of Allah must be above any formula (He is Indivisible). Balance of one in (142x19) +1 speaks of His Unity. Is it by design or a mere coincident? One cannot be sure at this stage.

But this was only the tip of the iceberg. Qur'an consists of 114 chapters which is 19x6. If you add all the sura numbers from one to 114 (i.e. 1+2+3+…….. 110+ 111+ 112+ 113+ 114) their sum total is 6555 which is also multiple of 19 i.e. 6555=19x345. It is also seen that only 113 suras begin with Bismillah. It is missing in sura Tauba. But, as if to complete the formula, this miss is compensated in sura Namal in which it occurs twice thus raising the number to 114 i.e. 19x6=114. Could this be a coincident also? Most likely not but still you can doubt.

Researchers were surprised to discover that the sum of serial numbers of all suras between at-Tauba (serial number 9 one at the start of which Bismillah is missing) and an-Namal (serial number 27, which has two Bismillah), 9+10+11+…….+26+27 = 342, is also a multiple of 19. Not only this, the researchers found the baffling fact that the number of words between the first bismillah in sura an-Namal and the second one is also 342, as if designed to fit this formula i.e. 342 = 19 x 18.

So many logical repetitions of the same phenomenon cannot be possibly a matter of coincidence or chance. It could be possible only by design. Will you then say that Muhammad Rasool Allah (صلى الله عليه وآله وسلم) who had not attended any school, and there were none in Arabia in those days, had himself designed and arranged the words, ayat, and chapters of a lengthy book like Qur'an in this mathematically fashion? But still there is a lot more on this subject.

65
THE FIRST REVELATION AND 19

This mind-boggling mathematical design is not limited to a few suras or a few words. It pervades throughout the Book. It appears as if the author of this Book had preplanned in His mind that He would write a book whose letters, words, ayaat and chapters will be arranged in a mathematical way to conform to the number 19. This is most startlingly evident in the first ever revelation from Allah *Subhana-Hu* to His Messenger (Peace be upon him). These are the famed five ayaat of sura al-Alaq,

اِقْرَأْ بِاسْمِ رَبِّكَ الَّذِىْ خَلَقَ ۞ خَلَقَ الْإِنْسَانَ مِنْ عَلَقٍ ۞ اِقْرَأْ وَرَبُّكَ الْاَكْرَمُ ۞ الَّذِىْ عَلَّمَ بِالْقَلَمِ ۞ عَلَّمَ الْإِنْسَانَ مَالَمْ يَعْلَمْ ۞

Read! With Name of your Rabb – Who created man from Alaq. Read, and your Rabb is the most Bountiful, Who taught by the Pen. Taught man that, he knew not.
[96(1-5)]

As can be seen, the Arabic text of this revelation consists of 19 words and 76 letters. Both numbers are a multiple of 19 (76 = 19 x 4). Moreover, this revelation is part of sura Al-Alaq, which is also composed of a total 19 ayaat only. More surprisingly, in the overall arrangement of the Holy Qur'an, this sura is placed at the 96th position out of the total 114 suras comprising of the entire Qur'an. Thus, there happen to be 95 (19 x 5) suras before Al-Alaq, and 19 suras after. Now prepare yourself for the most astonishing part: yes, the total sum of words comprising sura Al-Alaq is 304 – 19 x 16!!

Would any human author plan his or her book so painstakingly, according to the sophisticated mathematical design like this many centuries ago? Has anyone in the past, in any country of the world performed a similar feat? Why did Muhammad (Peace be upon him) do so. How did he achieve this symmetry? It is beyond human perception because it is not the work of any human being.

66
MIRACLE OF HAROOF-E-MUQQATIAT (SPECIAL INITIALS)

Doubtless what has been narrated so far, sounds quite strange. Let's carry on with more amazing examples of the sophisticated mathematical arrangement used in the Qur'an: some of the suras in the Holy Qur'an begin with certain Arabic alphabetic initials, which were unfamiliar even to contemporary Arabs. These are known as Haroof-e-Muqqatiat (حروف مقطعات). For example, sura Al-Baqara begins with the letters ا ل م, sura Yaseen with ى س. Seven suras begin with letters ح م. Sura Quaf begins with single letter ق, and sura Al-Qalam with ن only. Altogether, fourteen Arabic letters have been used for this purpose which is half of the total Arabic alphabet. And are arranged in fourteen different sets. Now, putting all the information above, together, if you add these numbers i.e. 14 (letters used as initials), 14 (different combinations) and 29 (number of suras beginning with these special initials), the total (14+14+29) is 57, again a multiple of 19!

In 1976 computers were first used to carry out mathematical analysis of the contents of the Holy Qur'an in USA[41]. It was then discovered that the occurrence of Haroof-e-Muqqatiat was as if deliberately designed to fit the mysterious code of 19. That means that the author of the Holy Qur'an must have counted all the letters and words of the Holy Qur'an and then adjusted them to obey the code of 19.

Take the simpler example which you can easily verify be simple counting also of sura al-Qalam. It begins with letter ن. The number of times that this letter occurs in this sura is 133, which is 19 x 7. Suras Araaf and Maryam are the two suras that begin with the letter ص. The number of times ص in these two suras is 152, again 19 x 8!

In sura Yaseen, (يس) (ي س), letter ي occurs 237 times and letter س 48 times. Sum of these two letters 237 + 48 = 285, is again (19 x 15) a multiple of 19!

Seven suras of the Holy Qur'an (40 to 46) begin with letter ح م. Total occurrence of the letter ح and letter م respectively, in these seven suras is 292 and 1,855, the sum of which is 2,147, also a multiple of 19 (19 x 113).

Sura ash-Shu'raa number 42 begins with letters ح م ع س ق, while sura aq-Quaf begins with the letter ق. If you count the letter ق in these two suras, it is found to occur 57 times in each sura, (57 = 19 x 3) for a total of 114 times – 19 x 6!!

---

[41] Rashid Khalifa "The Qur'an, the Visual Presentation of Miracle", Islamic Production, Arizona, USA, 1989

What is more is that sum of letter ق, which is the first letter of the word Qur'an, in every 19th ayat of every sura of the whole Qur'an, is 76, a multiple of 19!

67
FOOD FOR THOUGHT

In the above have been presented only a few examples of the mystery of 19 embedded in the structure of the Holy Qur'an. For further details on this intriguing topic, you may wish to consult reference 41 and 42, given below. Originally this discovery was announced in 1976 by an Egyptian scholar, Dr Rashid Khalifa in the US. Incidentally, that year was also a multiple of 19 (1976 = 19 x 104)! Since then more researchers have verified and enlarged upon the scope of this subject. The question however, remains, could Muhammad (Peace be upon him) or any other human author even today calculate and construct this code of 19 in the letters, words, phrases and suras of a voluminous Book like the Qur'an? Why would he do that? How could he possibly have done this?

We know for a fact that, Muhammad (Peace be upon him) never took formal education. He did not study mathematics. He had no computers, no calculators. He had no time to rest in his life either. Qur'an was no ordinary book. It was an anthology of discourses from Allah *Subhana-Hu* over 23 years, most of which period he was under ferocious attack by his enemies or given to preaching of Islam and fulfilling the immense responsibilities of leadership of the nascent emerging community of Muslims. However, all those who knew him, friends and foes alike, acknowledged him as an impeccably truthful and honest man. He never claimed that he was the author of the Qur'an. On the contrary, he always professed that the Qur'an was revealed to him from the Creator of the universe.

So re-think again, with all honesty about who could be the author of the Qur'an? Who could have built and designed such a large book on the basis of the intriguing mathematical code of the number 19? Even in this age of computers and information technology, such a feat will be extremely difficult to perform. Then how did Muhammad (Peace be upon him) manage it, if he is the one who authored the Qur'an? It is a challenge to everyone to reach to the correct decision.

If non-believers can rid themselves of their deep-seated prejudices – which is the real challenge for them and think objectively, it will immediately become as obvious as daylight to realize that it is not the work of a human, but the revelation from the Creator of the worlds, the living miracle of the last of the messengers of Allah *Subhana-Hu* to mankind.

As for the question, what was the necessity of designing the Holy Qur'an in this intricate mathematical fashion, we may suggest that it was done in order to provide infallible mathematical proof to modern man to believe in the true revelation from the Creator of the worlds. Alas, a large majority of mankind is still ignorant of this great truth! Of those who have known it, many simply say, 'strange, very strange, indeed', but do not approach it for guidance. The Holy Qur'an had predicted this attitude in ayat 2 of sura al-Quaf which says,
> **"So the unbelievers say: This is a strange thing" 50(2).**

68
NUMERICAL SYMMETRY OF OCCURRENCE OF SOME SPECIAL WORDS IN THE HOLY Qur'an

The Holy Qur'an declares that Allah has created everything in paired symmetry (sura Yaseen, ayat 36). It comes as no surprise therefore that a similar symmetry has been maintained in the choice of certain key words in the Divine Book. Here are some fascinating examples:[42]

1. Duniya & Akhirat (الدنيا وآخرة): The word 'duniya' relates to the earthly world and akhirat (آخرة) relates to the hereafter. Thus, they are the names of two complementary worlds. It is surprising that each one of these words occurs 115 times in the Holy Qur'an.

2. Days in a Month: The word 'youm' (يوم) means day. One is surprised to see that it occurs exactly 365 times in the Holy Qur'an! In its plural forms, 'youmain' (يومين) or 'ayyam' (ايام) it occurs thirty times – equal to the average number of days in a month. Even more strikingly, the number of times that the word 'shaher' (شهر), which means a month in Arabic, occurs, exactly 12, times being the number of months in a year.

3. Shaitaan & Angels (الشيطان) - (الملائكه): Shaitaan and angels are two of Allah's creations with opposing characteristics. In the spiritual world shaitaan

---

[42] A. Rashid Seyal "Poetic Stance of the Holy Qur'an", 2006, 16 1-3 Berty Drive, Bloomington, USA (www.authorhinge.co.uk); also, Dr Tariq-Al-Swaiden of Ikhwan al-Muminon, Egypt

represents the evil, whereas angels represent pure goodness. It is also surprising therefore, to see that the number of occurrence of the word shaitaan (شيطان) in the entire Qur'an is exactly equal to the number of occurrence of the word malaika (ملائكه), each 88 times.

4. Reward and Forgiveness (مغفرة – الجزا): The spiritual system of accountability is based on reward and forgiveness. Thus, the number of occurrence of the words al-jaza(الجزا) , which means payment or reward, is 117, while the word maghfirah(مغفرة) which means forgiveness, occurs exactly twice as many times, ie 234. It might appear that Allah *Subhana-Hu* is twice as likely to incline toward forgiveness.

5. Jannat (جنت)) and Jahannam (جهنم): These are two opposing worlds of the hereafter. Jannat ie paradise, is the sumptuous abode of the righteous, while Jahannam(جهنم) ie hell, is the destiny of the wretched, unforgivable ones in the hereafter. Both these terms appear exactly 77 times in the Qur'an.

6. Righteous (ابرار) & Wicked ((فجار: The word abraar (ابرار) which means the righteous ones, is used 6 times in the Qur'an. Its opposite is the word al-fujjar (الفجار), meaning the wicked ones. This occurs 3 times, exactly half.

7. Wine (خمر) & Intoxication (سكارى): The word khamar (خمر) refers to all types of wine and saqara (سكارى) means intoxication, an effect of wine. Both these terms occur 6 times each in the Qur'an.

8. Love (المحبه) & Obedience(اطاعت) : The word al-muhabbah (المحبه), which means love and the word ataa't (اطاعت) , meaning obedience, represent the attitude of true Muslim, as he tends toward the latter given the ascent in the former, both in relation to his relationship with his Creator. Each occurs 107 times.

9. Disaster (مصيبة) & Thanks (الشكر): The word musibat (مصيبة) means disaster; and the ash-shuker (الشكر), means thanks. Each of these occurs 75 times in the text of the Holy Qur'an.

10. Sun (الشمس)& Light (نور): The word ash-shams (الشمس) means the sun, and noor(نور) means light. Quite surprisingly, each of these words is used 33 times in the Qur'an.

11. Man & Woman(الرجل و المراء) : The word for man(الرجل) and the word for women(المراة) , occur 23 times each in the Book. Surprisingly enough, this is the same number as the number of x- and y-chromosomes in the male sperm and the female ovum.

12. Life (الحياة) & Death (الموت): Life (الحياة) and death (الموت) are two contrasting realities. They also happen to occur exactly in equal number in the Qur'an – 145 times each.

13. Sight (بصارت) & Insight (بصيرت): The words sight(بصارت) and insight (بصيرت) are

complementary. Each one is mentioned 148 times in the Holy Qur'an.

14. Zaka (زكوة) and Barakah (بركة): The word zakat (compulsory Islamic tax) and barakah (blessings of Allah), form a complementary pair; so it happens that each has occurred 32 times in the Holy Qur'an.

15. As-salam (السلام) used for peace and the word at-tayibaat (الطيبة) (delicacies) occur 50 times each.

16. The word khayanat (خيانت) which means treachery occurs 16 times. In the same number occurs the word khabeeth (خبيث) which means disgustful wicked.

17. Al-yasr (اليسر) (ease) and al-usr (العسر) (difficulty), each occurs 36 times. At 94(5-6) in the Holy Qur'an, Allah *Subhana-Hu* does ordain that both these states of affair go hand in hand.

18. Words jihad (جهاد) (holy war) and Muslimeen (مسلمين) each occur 41 times, as if one is not complete without the other.

19. The word Barr (بر) which means dry land, occurs 13 times; and the word Baher (بحر) which means land under water occurs 32 times. Ratio between 13 and 32 is the same as the actual ratio of dry and under water land on earth.

The important question here is that if Muhammad (Peace be upon him) was the real author of the Qur'an, how could he have adjusted such a massive book in such a fine manner as to achieve the incredible symmetry shown above. Did he have the time and the means to do this? And to what end, especially when he himself is not even known to have claimed this remarkable credit. Then what did he stand to achieve in creating an amazing product without need credit during his life time? Indeed no other author in human history is known to have achieved something like this. The only plausible answer to these questions is that the Holy Qur'an is not that the work of a man. It is just simply a revelation from Allah, the Creator of the worlds. As for its significance Muslims scholars need to ponder over it.

69
THE MIRACULOUS ARRANGEMENT OF THE HOLY QUR'AN

The Holy Qur'an is the only revealed book left today with mankind in its original shape as delivered to the last Messenger of Allah (Peace be upon him), more than fourteen hundreds years ago. Whenever an ayat was revealed to the Prophet (Peace be upon him) he personally directed the Qur'anic scribes to write it down at specific locations in a specific sura. This process continued for almost 23 years.

Thus the Messenger of Allah himself (Peace be upon him) compiled the Qur'an in its current format under divine guidance. He and many of his followers also remembered the entire Qur'an, in its present arrangement by heart. Ever now there are millions of Muslims around the world who know the whole Book by memory, accurate down to each punctuation mark. After the Messenger of Allah (Peace be upon him) passed away, the first caliph of Islam, Abu

Bakar (may Allah be pleased with him) ordered the compilation of the Qur'an in a standard bound format. Since Islam was spreading rapidly at that stage, the third Caliph, Usman (may Allah be pleased with him), authorised several authentic copies of the original standard book and placed them in each provincial capitals as a reference for the general public. One of these copies used by the caliph himself is said to be still available in Istanbul's great mosque. Thus the Holy Qur'an is preserved to this day exactly as it was arranged by the Messenger of Allah (Peace be upon him).

70
DIVISION OF THE HOLY QUR'AN INTO CHAPTERS AND PARTS

The Holy Qur'an is arranged in 114 suras of various lengths, but it is not arranged in the chronological order of its original revelations. Some of the ayaat revealed in Madina for instance, may be part of earlier Makkan suras. In its general arrangement however, the longer suras take precedence of location and the smaller ones follow later. However, there are certain exceptions to this rule; the first sura, al-Fatiha, consisting of seven ayaat, precedes the second and the longest sura of the Qur'an, al-Baqara, containing 286 ayaat. The Book is also divided into thirty parts, known as a 'juz', each of which is given an individual name. The question that has frequently been asked is, whether this arrangement is arbitrary or is in accordance with Divine instructions to the Holy Prophet (Peace be upon him). Some possible answers to this question are:

1. The Qur'an is arranged in its present form for aesthetic reasons, and to facilitate reading and memorizing.
2. The longer suras have been placed first because they deal with social issues of practical importance, and the shorter suras are placed later, on account of their stress on spiritual development of man and on life hereafter, or that.
3. The arrangement is simply haphazard, devoid of any logic or reason.

The reader can figure out that it means that there is no satisfactory answer to the original question. The unsatisfactory responses above, beg the query that if the Qur'an is truly a revelation from the Creator of the universe, as it is beyond any doubt, then it cannot be illogically arranged. The Qur'anic arrangement into chapters and parts must have a deeper meaning that we haven't managed to fathom. But what is it? The answer to this question was found in the staggering discovery of the graphical structure of the Holy Qur'an.

If you list the 114 suras of the Qur'an in cumulative order, against the 30 juz (parts), and then draw a graph between these two quantities, suddenly an amazing relationship emerges between them. This is shown in the figure given herein. Serial numbers of Suras run along the Y-axis and serial numbers of the parts are along the X-axis (For example, at the end of part 16, already 20 suras have begun). The points when joined together form almost a perfect curve. This is rare, to say the least. Even in the case of accurately recorded results, quantities are generally scattered around a mean curve. But in this case we find a perfect harmony, beautiful to a scientist's eye. It clearly has a special mathematical message, proving that the arrangement of the Qur'an into chapters and parts is not ordinary, but very meaningful. There is absolutely no question of any haphazardness in this arrangement.

RELATIONSHIP BETWEEN SURA NUMBERS AND JUZ NUMBERS

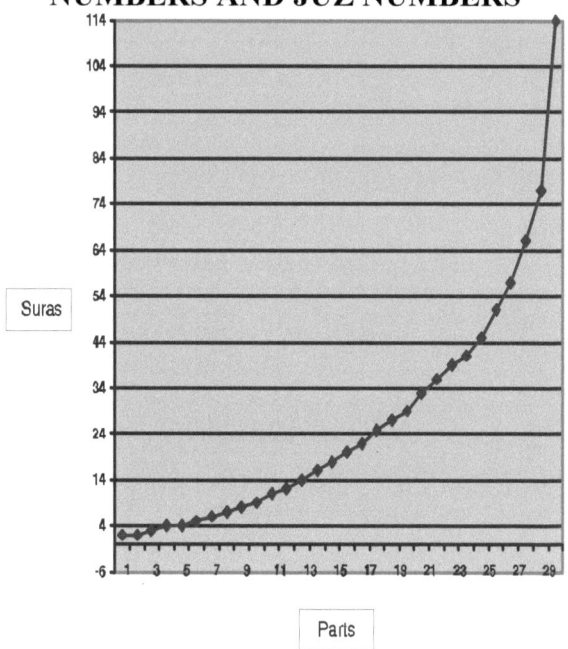

TABLE - 1

ARRANGEMENT OF THE QURAN INTO SURAS AND PARTS

Serial Number of	Serial Number of the SURAS till the end
X	Y
1	2
2	2
3	3
4	4
5	4
6	5
7	6
8	7
9	8
10	9
11	11
12	12
13	14
14	16
15	18
16	20
17	22
18	25
19	27
20	29
21	33
22	36
23	39
24	41
25	45
26	51
27	57
28	66
29	77
30	114

X - Serial Number of the JUZ
Y – Serial Number of SURAS at the end of a JUZ

71
SIGNIFICANCE

As we analyze the graphical arrangement of suras and the parts of the Qur'an we find out, that the curve first runs parallel to the x-axis, but it never touches zero. Then it picks up gradually, finally shooting up exponentially. At the end it goes up almost vertically.

This behaviour may thus signify the spiritual development of a believer as he progresses through the Holy Qur'an. The fact that the curve does not start from zero may indicate that some basic potential for spiritual development exists in everyone. Even the non-believers have a basic instinct and awareness of Allah *Subhana-Hu* to start with.

As the student progresses through the Qur'an, his/her spirit begins to ascend toward Allah *Subhana-Hu*. At the beginning, the rate of development is slow. Then suddenly it picks up. For example, one attains only about 50% development on reaching the 26th juz of the Qur'an. Then it accelerates, reaching 100% by the end of the Qur'an.

The reason for this phenomenon may be that initial suras of the Holy Qur'an lay a great deal of stress on the outward reformation of the individual and the society. They contain Do's and Don'ts about Islamic law and generally educate believers to develop a strong moral personality that is essential for their subsequent spiritual development. Once the individual has disciplined his/her outward life in terms of the injunctions of Divine revelation, he then becomes capable of receiving the full light of the Holy Qur'an. Hence the spiritual development of a believer is geometrically accelerated toward the final stages of the Book of Allah.

One may ask, was it possible for the Prophet himself (Peace be upon him) to design such a mathematical arrangement? We all know that mathematics was in its infancy during the prophet's day. The concept of graphs or complex functions did not even exist. How could any human author at that time arrange a textbook according to a graphical function like this then?

There can be no possible explanation to this question except that the Qur'an is not the work of a man, but the revelation from the Creator of the universe.

It is not only its contents, but even the arrangement of the Book of Allah into chapters and parts, manifests a Divine design (may Allah be praised).

> *"Praise be to Allah, Who revealed over His Servant the Book, and has allowed there in no crookedness." 18 (1)*

> *"Do they not consider the Qur'an? Had it been from other than Allah, they would have found therein much discrepancy."*
> *4 (82)*

Part IV

The Spirit of the Islam

72
DISCOVERING ISLAM

"Let there be no compulsion in religion, as the Truth stands out clear from false hood. Whoever thus rejects evil and believes in Allah has grasped the most Trust worthy hand-hold that never breaks. And Allah hears and knows all things". (Al-Baqra Ayat 256)

Have you ever asked, "Why am I a Muslim, or a Christian or a Hindu or of any other Faith"? Answer is quite clear "It is because of the parents, for that you had no choice. They had also inherited their faith from their parents. Thus what ever your religion, it is due to inheritance. Can any one then claim superiority on this account? Why should a Just God reward or punish some one due to the religion given to him/her at birth.

More are less traditional religions over the time have been polluted by the selfish interests of the priestly classes, who tend to pose themselves as the intermediary between Man and God. The religions gradually become profession for the priests and thus lose the Prophetic spirit. However, it does not provide excuse for the believers not to seek for the Truth. In reality, all of us are answerable to our Creator, for our efforts to discover the Path leading to Him. If in our normal lives we are so much choosy for everything, then how could we be excused for our non-serious attitude toward the philosophy of life? If God exists, and He does, then it should be the most important decision of our lives. We must rediscover consciously religion for us.

Truth of the matter is that all of us are accountable to God for each and every action of our life on earth. Lest we make excuses in the Hereafter that we were caught unaware, Allah *Subhana-Hu* has laid down specific criteria of what is right and what is wrong for us. To teach it, He sent His especially chosen teachers to every nation on earth. They are called prophets. Some of the more well known of them are: Adam, Noah, Abraham, Isaac, Ismael, Jacob, Moses, and Jesus Christ, (may peace be upon them all). When humanity had developed enough and could preserve the purity of Message of Allah in writing for good He sent His last messenger Muhammad (Peace be upon him), to consolidate and complete the teachings of all the earlier prophets for all times to come. This system of life is called Islam. It is not the religion invented by Mohammad (Peace be upon him) but is completion of the mission of the earlier prophets.

It is most unfortunate that beautiful image of Islam has been badly tarnished by its enemies through their false propaganda and misinformation campaigns. However even more unfortunate than this is that some of the so called Muslims falsely depict Islam for the sake of their own vested interests. Added to this is the ignorance of the large majority of the Muslims by birth of their own religion. Combined together they have made it very difficult for the seekers of truth to receive the Divine light for their salvation. In the following pages an attempt has been made to rediscover the spirit of Islam. If someone can get rid of the inherited prejudices, he/she will be realty surprised to see the beauty of Islam for the peace and progress of mankind.

73
THE UNIVERSAL NATURAL RELIGION

Islam fundamentally is to believe in one God, with all His attributes and submit to Him humbly with the belief in the life Hereafter and Resurrection for accountability of our transient earthly sojourn. Salvation lies in developing our personalities on the pattern of the attributes of Allah *Subhana-Hu* to earn His pleasure, and win back the lost Jannat (Paradise). Thus a true Muslim is not only a "Man of God", but "God like Man" at his/her own humble pedestal, the ideal example of which is the last Messenger of Allah (Peace be upon him).

The fact that Islam is the continuation of the religion of the earlier prophets is clarified by the following commandment of Allah in sura Ash-Shu'raa of the Holy Qur'an.

> *He has ordained for you the 'Deen' (ie way of life) revealed unto you same which He had commanded unto Noah, and that which He had commanded unto Abraham, and Moses, and Jesus. Therefore you also, establish the (same) Deen (for Allah), and be not divided therein [42(13)]*

Being a Muslim therefore means that he/she is as much a believer in Jesus (Peace be upon him) as a Christian is; or in Moses as a true Jew. This is the natural religion for man about which Allah *Subhana-Hu* says in sura Ar-Roum, ayat 30 of the Holy Qur'an.

> *And so set your face steadfastly towards the Deen (of Allah), turning away from all that is false, to the natural disposition which Allah has instilled into Man, not to*

> *allow any change to corrupt what Allah has thus created – This is the right way of life; but most people know not [30(30)]*

Islam is thus the religion most suited to the nature of man. Reward for the one who follows it truly is spiritual elevation to become the "Vicegerent of Allah on Earth" – the very purpose of man's creation, as revealed on ayat 30 of sura Al-Baqara,

> ***Behold, your Rabb said to the angels, "I will create a vicegerent on earth" [2(30)]***

Islam clarifies that every child is born with this natural potential, and it has come to show man the guidance to raise him/her to this exalted status.

74
THE ESSENCE OF ISLAM

In its basic philosophy Islam teaches that universe is created for man. In turn he/she is made for the Creator of the universe. Thus man is not the product of universe but the very reason for it. As such the essence of Islam is "service" to Allah and "service" to His creatures. In this philosophy the obligations of the one, are the rights of the others. They are of two types:-

1. Obligations to Allah, the Creator (حقوق الله)
2. Obligations to creatures of Allah (حقوق العباد)

As a result of the fulfilment of these obligations, Islam promises "Peace at all levels". Infact, dictionary meaning of the word 'Islam' is 'Peace" and code word of a Muslim is (اسلام عليكم) i.e. "peace be upon you". When two Muslims get together, each one must try to surpass in his/her greetings of "Peace". Islam also means "Submission to Allah". Thus Peace plan of Islam is "Peace through submission to Allah", the scope of which is very wide. To the least it consists of the following fundamentals:

- To be at peace with your Creator,
- To be at peace with your own self,
- To be at peace with your neighbour, and
- To be at peace with all other creations of Allah *Subhana-Hu*.

Since the converse of peace is "Mischief" (فساد) i.e. to engage in destabilizing the natural equilibrium established by Allah *Subhana-Hu* on earth, for the sake of peace, where required, a Muslim is supposed to fight with the mischievous evil forces of exploitation, tyranny, ignorance and greed. The basic principle is revealed is ayat 205, sura Al-Baqra,

> "Allah does not like any type of mischief"   2(205).

Thus it is obligatory on every believer not only to dissociate himself/herself from all causes which may damage peace but practically to fight for it. Technically it is called Jehaad (جهاد) i.e. the struggle against evil to establish peace. Both complement each other. It is the highest act of worship, and an essential obligation on every Muslims about which the Holy Qur'an says in sura Aal-e-Imran, ayat 110 **"You are the best of the people, as** *you come out for mankind to establish what is good; and prevent what is evil……", (110).* Thus every believer must work to promote peace, and fight with evil, as the Qur'an says, *"continuous mischief is worse than a (temporary) fight" 2(217).*

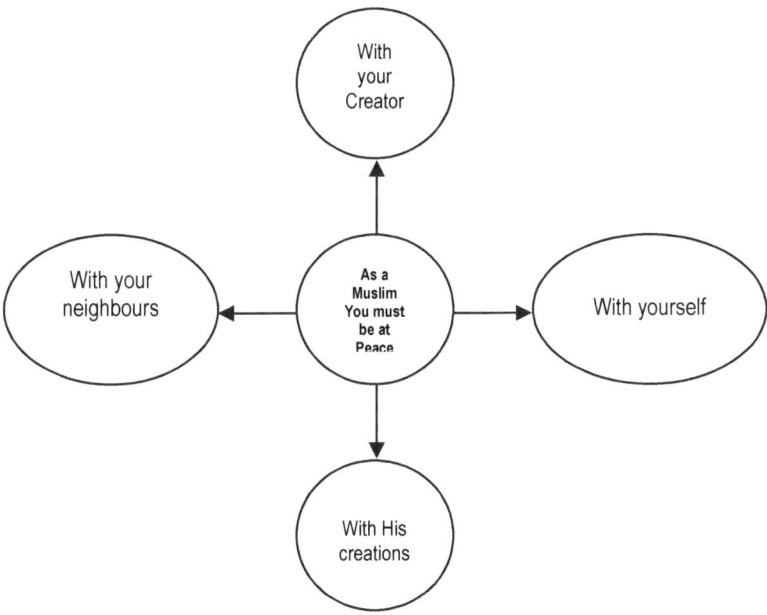

Fig. 1: Peace Plan of Islam through "the Submission to the Will of Allah"

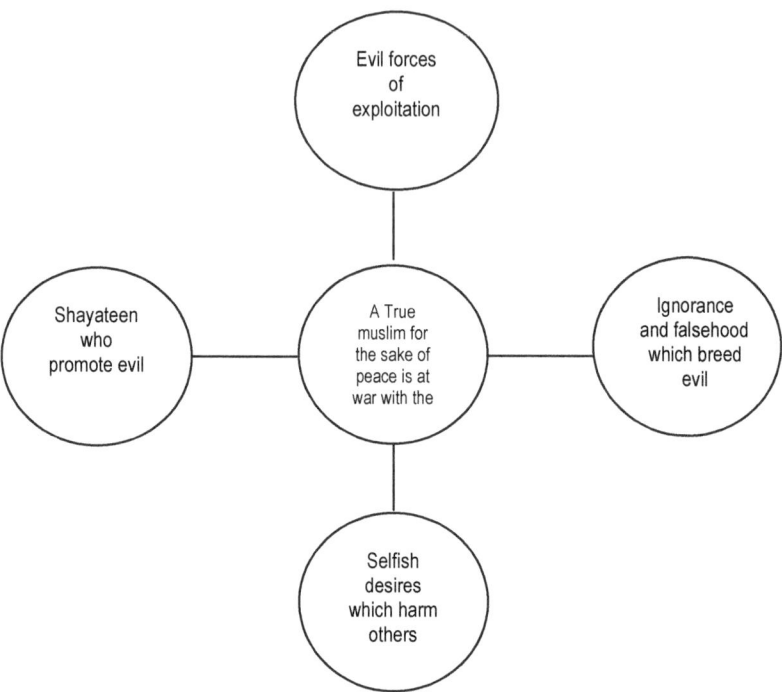

Fig 1B: War against evil trying to damage peace

In the following we shall highlight some of the salient features of this multidimensional approach to Peace. It is most comprehensively explained in the Holy Qur'an and was practically demonstrated by the Messenger of Allah, Muhammad (Peace be upon him) and his revered companions as the main objective of the blessed Islamic rule i.e. "Khilafat-e-Rashida" established by them.

75
PEACE WITH YOUR CREATOR

To be at peace with our Creator means to always remain conscious of Him and strive constantly to earn His love and pleasure and assign no partners to Him. It depends upon building a staunch, unshakable belief in Allah *Subhana-Hu* with all His attributes; Practically it means complete submission to Him; thus moulding one's life according to His attributes demonstrated by the exemplary human role model of the last Messenger of Allah (Peace be upon him).

It is obligatory on every Muslim to demonstrate his/her resolve of submission to Allah *Subhana-Hu* by the minimum acts of worship. These are the five times a day salat (prayers), fasting in the month of Ramadan, the compulsory payment of zakat (due to the poor), and at least once in lifetime pilgrimage to the House of Allah at Makkah, originally built by Prophet Adam (Peace be upon him) and latter re-built on its foundation by the Prophet Abraham (Peace be upon him), over 4000 years ago.

Adherence to these practices entitles one to join the club of Islam as its basic member. Spiritual promotions and achievements within it will depend upon how well we do for the rest of the "Peace program of Islam".

76
PEACE WITH YOURSELF

The Islamic philosophy, to be at peace with your own self, relies profoundly on giving peace to others. It starts with your own family. In the Holy Qur'an Allah Subhana-Hu says; **"O, those who believe, save yourself and your family from the hellfire (Sura Al-Baqra)** This is achievable through a strong commitment to Islam, by becoming as useful member of the society as possible, loving and a helping hand for everyone as per the example of the prophet of Islam (Peace be upon him), Allah says in the Holy Qur'an, He is blessing for all the worlds, therefore his true follower cannot be but blessing for his/her own environment at least. He/she will never wilfully hurt others, and will be ever ready to cultivate loving and caring relations with others particularly with in the family. At the personal level he/she will try to surpass with others in doing the right deeds, maintaining clean thoughts, pleasant disposition and in faithfully adopting the do's and the don'ts revealed by Allah in the Holy Qur'an.

In this respect the guidance provided in sura al-Asar, ayaat 1-5 is exceedingly contemplative, **"I swear by passing time that man by nature is apt to loss, accepting those who believe in Allah, do good deeds, and help each other on the Right Path; And council each other to persevere with patience in the way of Allah"**.

It means that personal belief and good deeds are not enough for the spiritual peace to you. It also depends upon the fulfilment of your social obligations. Thus a good Muslim must be active member of the society who stands for the right and helps the needy. He has a caring personality, dutiful in dealings with others, and takes pleasure in giving others more than in getting back from them.

77
PEACE WITH YOUR NEIGHBOUR

To be at peace with his/her neighbour is an intrinsic obligation of every true Muslim. The messenger of Allah (Peace be upon him) warned, **"You can't be a Muslim if the honour and property of others is not safe from you."** Thus, even aggressive gestures backbiting, jealousy, and use of abusive language are prohibited. If they relate to your neighbour they are then terrible sins.

At 107(4-7) in the Holy Qur'an Allah *Subhana-Hu* warns the worshippers who are not kind to their neighbours,

> *So woe to the worshippers, who are neglectful of their prayers, those who (worship but) to be seen (by others), and refuse (to meet) neighbourly needs. 107(4-7)*

The prophet Muhammad (Peace be upon him) also told Muslims, **'If your neighbour sleeps hungry, or if he is sick and not looked after, your prayers will not be accepted'**. Omar, the second rightly guided caliph of Islam (may Allah be pleased with him) set the standard by declaring, **'even if a dog dies of hunger at the banks of river Euphrates (a river in Iraq), Omar is responsible in Madinah'**.

Looking after orphans, widows and destitute in the neighbourhood is an obligatory duty of every Muslim. In this connection sura al-Ma'oon, ayaat 1-3 provide a decisive ruling **"Have you seen of him who rejects the Deen (Islam). He is the one who repulses the orphan and cares not for feeding the destitute"**. In view of such fateful imperative, stating the conclusive primacy of caring for the orphans and the destitute amounts tantamount to a rejection of one's deen, it is a wonder that the thoughtful of the Muslims can ever dare to contravene this commandment.

The Messenger of Allah (Peace be upon him) defined neighbourhood as comprising of forty homes on all sides, i.e. 1600 houses all around. Thus one after the other, all people on earth are each other's neighbours and covered by the neighbourly peace plan of Islam. The general rule about neighbourly behaviour, ordained by the prophet of Allah (Peace be upon him) is, that **"The best of the mankind is the one who is the most useful to them."**

78
PEACE WITH NATURE

The Holy Qur'an teaches man to respect nature and maintain its beauty and therefore is forbidden to pollute or spoil peace of earth. It is emphasized to preserve the equilibrium that Allah *Subhana-Hu* Himself created and to acknowledge the rights of all living beings created by Him, to flourish and thrive.

In this respect the first and the foremost requirement of Islam is the maintenance of the earth's environment. Allah *Subhana-Hu* says in the Holy Qur'an, **'don't spoil and create mischief in the Earth after that it has been set right' 7(85).** Thus it is the sacred duty enjoined upon every Muslim, to keep the environment clean and not to upset its inherent equilibrium. That is why in the past, good Muslim scientists refused to invent harmful things, even at the orders of the caliph.

With respect to nature the fundamental philosophy of Islam as told by the prophet of Allah (Peace be upon him) is that **'the creations of Allah are like His family'** (الخلق عيال الله). Through various of his saying as well as his deeds, the prophet suggested to grow trees and not to needlessly chop and burn plants; to look after the wild and domestic animals; to contribute in the cleanliness of public spaces; clearing roads and lanes of obstacles; and not to waste earthly resources. It is prohibited to waste resources, even if one owns them in plenty. He went so far as to say, **"don't waste water even for ablution, though you may be sittings at the banks of a river"**. He taught Muslims to respect nature in the belief that whatever Allah has made on earth is beautiful, and that we owe responsibility to maintain that beauty. He (Peace be upon him) said in one of his sayings, **"Allah is beautiful and He loves beauty"**. Thus maintenance of natural beauty, as far as possible, is a mandatory on every true Muslim.

79
TO BE AT WAR WITH EVIL

As every believer in Islam is duty bound to promote peace to preserve it, it is also obligatory on him/her to oppose the evil forces which disturb peace. Thus he/she must fight against all forms of exploitation and oppression. Indeed accomplishing good is not possible without the struggle against evil. A true Muslim will not let evil flourish around and take over the goodness. They are fundamentally ordained to oppose the force of exploitation by all possible means: till to the finish, as Allah orders in the Holy Qur'an. *"Fight them till the end of mischief" (sura Infaal, ayat 39).* In Islam tolerance of evil is synonymous to participating in it.

General principle is pointed out in ayat 75 of sura. An-Nisa **"And why should you not fight in the cause of Allah and of those who being weak, are ill treated (and oppressed)? Men, women and children whose cry is "Our Lord (Rabb)! Rescue us from this town whose people are oppressors; and raise for us from you, the one who will protect (us); And send for us from you who will help (us)" 4(75)**

80
SPIRITUAL PHILOSOPHY OF ISLAM

Once the peace is established spiritual development starts rapidly in the peaceful environment. Then the mankind will have time, opportunity and mood to achieve the higher realities of life.

For his/her spiritual development, the action plan of the life of a Muslim rests upon Islam's philosophy of unity of the fundamental realities; and equality of mankind. This is:-

1. Unity of Allah, that there is no god but Him only, with out any partners, father or son etc.

2. Unity of the institution of Prophet-hood, that Mohammad is the last of the messengers of Allah,

3. Unity of the Message of Allah, that Qur'an is the exactly preserved last revealed book of Allah,

integrating the fundamental teachings of all the pervious prophets.

4. Unity of the purpose of life, To serve the Creator and His creatures

5. Equality of mankind that all human beings are bothers and sisters, as the progeny of Adam and Eve (PBUT)

Belief in the unity of Allah *Subhana-Hu* leads to the liberation from all false gods. This is the starting point in our journey to the highest realities of Islam which we cannot comprehend otherwise. Belief in the unity of the institution of Prophet-hood and unity of the message of Allah ends confusion, clarifies the visions and opens before us the Right Path leading to Jannat (Paradise).

Belief in the unity of mankind focuses on the commonality in mankind, all being the progeny of Adam (Peace be upon him). As such all are equal in terms of human rights. Any claims of superiority on the basis of colour, clan or race are spurious. The last Messenger of Allah (Peace be upon him) taught that mankind is like the family of Gods each one being the honoured member of this family, so respect each other. We must therefore, concentrate on the singular purpose of life that is service to our Creator and service to His creatures faithfully.

The pragmatic fulfilment this philosophy rests upon the unconditional declaration of the creed of Islam, a statement called the *kalama-e-tayyaba* (كلمہ طیبہ).

لا اله الآالله محمّد الرسول الله

"There is no god but Allah, and Muhammad is the Messenger of Allah."

The declaration of this fundamental formulation of Islam entails making the following three commitments:

- Proclamation of *'la ilaha'*, (لا اله) 'there is no god', is liberation from servitude, physical as well as spiritual defiance of false deities, and the renunciation of all previously held beliefs, notions, ideas, customs and philosophies, if found inconsistent with Islam.

- Proclamation of *'ill-al-Allah'*, (الاألله) 'except Allah' is the resolution to obey and serve only Allah, to glorify His name and mould our lives in accord with His revelations, i.e. the Holy Qur'an.

- By proclaiming *'Muhammad Ur-Rasool-Allah'* (محمّد الرسول الله) (Peace be upon him), we deposit our faith in Muhammad, the last prophet of Allah, as the supreme leader of all mankind, guide, teacher and the role model for all dimensions of life, with the Holy Qur'an as the source of guidance, the Book revealed to him for the guidance of mankind.

The one who believes in this philosophy sincerely and tries to mould accordingly, his/her all activities and pursuits are acts of worship. There is nothing secular for them. It is all sacred. In their spiritual journey they aim to qualify for the proud title of being 'The Vicegerent of God in Earth'.

81
A TRUE MUSLIM – THE VICEGERENT OF ALLAH *SUBHANA-HU*

Islam teaches us that man is not some insignificant accidental product of universe, but in fact is the exclusive reason for its creations. He is the actual design basis of the universe. In this respect Allah says in the Holy Qur'an, **"Indeed, We have bestowed Mankind with honour"** (ولقد كرمنا بنى آدم). Thus all mankind, believers and non believers alike as human beings, are honourable in the Sight of Allah *Subhana-Hu*. When a true Muslim submits unconditionally and wholeheartedly to Allah, he is the pride of the universe.

Qualification for becoming the Vicegerent of God on Earth, demands that believers must aim to develop their personalities in accordance with to the attributes of Allah *Subhana-Hu* Himself. *He is not only to be the Man of God, but at his own humble level his/her ideal is to become like Him, by adopting His attributes,* (اسماء الحسنة) *(the beautiful names).* In this respect, the ideal example is of Muhammad, the Messenger of Allah (Peace be upon him). He asked **believers to mould their personalities in accordance with the attributes of Allah. He said** تخلقوا باخلاق الله. The degree of our closeness to Him depends upon the extent to which we colour ourselves in the Colour of Allah, as said in sura Al-Baqra ayat 138, of the Holy Qur'an;

> (Take) Hue of Allah! And what will be better hue (to life) than that of Allah's (Hue). And (Muslim) truly submit to Him only". 2(138)

Such a Muslim is the pride of creation, truly successful and respectable in this life and in the life hereafter. For him/her there is no fear and no tension (ولا خوف اليهم ولا هم يحزنون) any where.

PERSONALITY OF A TRUE MUSLIM

Following are some of the attributes of Allah *Subhana-Hu*. As said above, the goal for believers should be to adopt these attributes as much as possible and thus mould their personalities accordingly. The more you proactive the attributes of Allah, the nearer you will be to Him:

a. Allah embodies Absolute Kindness and Mercy: So a true Muslim must always be kind and merciful.

b. Allah is the Absolute Love: So a true Muslim must possess a loving personality.

c. Allah is the Supreme Creator: A true Muslim must also be continuously engaged in creative activities.

d. Allah is the Absolute Giver: Thus a Muslim must also possess a benevolent hand.

e. Allah is the Ultimate Source of Goodness: So a believer must also endeavour to attain excellence in his pursuits of life.

f. Allah is the Ever-forgiving and the Most Tolerant: So a true Muslim must also be forgiving and tolerant.

g. Allah is All-Knowing: So a true Muslim must also be keen to develop knowledge throughout life.

h. Allah is All-Wise: So the believer must also exhibit wisdom and a balanced personality.

i. Allah is the Ever Seeing, Ever Listening: Like Him a Muslim, at his own humble human level, must also keep his eyes and ears open, be a keen observer and a good listener.

j. Allah is the Absolutely Just: So a true Muslim must always be just and fair in all his conduct and undertakings.

k. Allah is the Most Honourable: A true believer in Allah *Subhana-Hu* must also be self respecting and honourable and never let himself be disgraceful.

l. Allah is the Absolute Helper. So a Muslim must also be a helping hand possessed of a considerate, caring and sharing nature.

m. Allah is the Absolute Sustainer and Nourisher of everything: Thus a true Muslim must also be a concerned citizen, mindful of the needs of others and be ready to feed the hungry.

n. Allah loves cleanliness: So a Muslim must also always remain in a state of physical and spiritual purity, devoid of contamination.

o. Allah hates transgressors and oppressors: So a believer must also oppose oppression and transgression based on the criteria set in the Book of Allah.

p. Allah hates the proud and arrogant: So a true Muslim must remain humane and humble, and treat other people with respect without exhibiting a midget of pride.

q. Allah hates liars: So a true Muslim is inextricably bound to truth.

r. Allah hates the miserly: So will a Muslim be generous and magnanimous and be ever prepared to large heartedly spend in Allah's way.

s. Allah hates those who preach what they do not do themselves: So must a true Muslim disdain hypocrisy.

t. Allah hates wastage: So a true Muslim must avoid wasting resources.

u. Allah is the Most Beneficent: So a true Muslim must also try to be as beneficial as possible towards all creations of Allah.

v. Allah is the Originator and Inventor of everything: So the believer must also be dynamic, thoughtful and courageous in trying out new ideas and in creating new projects.

w. **Allah is Peace:** So will a believer must also be peaceful, and always endeavouring and contributing in promoting peace.

x. **Allah loves the trustworthy and those who fulfil their pledge:** Therefore a true Muslim must also always fulfil his word and be entirely trustworthy.

y. **Allah loves those who remain steadfast against kufr (disbelief):** So a believer will never compromise on Islam.

In conclusion, we may say that a true Muslim does not only belong to Allah, he represents Him on earth. He embodies His attributes and thus at his/her own humble level endeavours to be like his/her Creator. In this striving he becomes the pride of the universe and a source of blessing for every thing. In return, the creatures of the environment salute them, angels pray for them, and Allah showers His pleasures on them.

83
THE MAN OF THE HOLY QUR'AN

Endeavour of a true Muslim is to become the "Man of the Holy Qur'an" about whom Allah says in it:-

> *(Muslims are) such they as remember Allah, standing sitting, and reclining; and*

in contemplation reflect into the creation of the heaven and the earth. [3(191)]

The prophet (Peace be upon him) is reported to have said, **"A Muslim whose today is the same as was his yesterday is a loser"**. For a Muslim this saying of the prophet entails to ensure that every day of his life must be better than the day before. That is the test of the strength of his belief in Islam. If a believer stands still, remains dormant, this might be an indication that something is lacking in his understanding of Islam. He/she will also then quickly lose their status of being the vicegerent on earth.

A true Muslim has a dynamic personality, who remains constantly engaged in the following three pursuits,

1. Zikr (ذكر)

2. Fikr (فكر)

3. Taskheer (تسخير)

These qualities are essential for continuous upward development in the physical as well the spiritual worlds of man. Allah *Subhana-Hu* showers His blessings upon those who endeavour in these pursuits. In the following we shall explain them briefly.

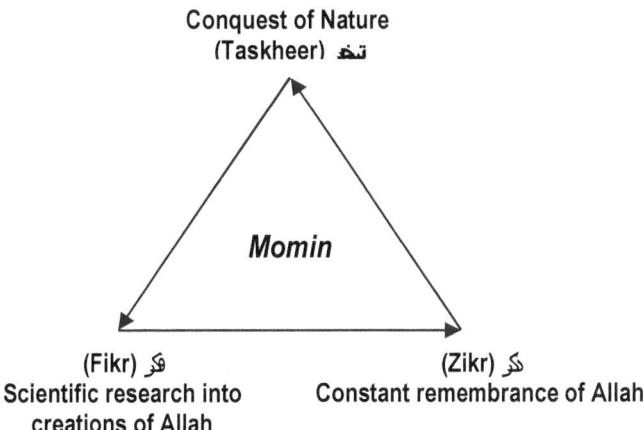

Zikr (ذکر) means to always be conscious of the presence of Allah *Subhana-Hu*, and obey Him in all walks of life. On this, Muslims are commanded in the Holy Qur'an; **"O! You who believe! Remember Allah in your remembrance always" 33(41).** In sura al-Muzammil, believers are asked, **"Remember and Glorify the Name of your Rabb with full devotion".**

This does not mean mechanical repetition of His Holy Name, but to live by keeping Him always in your thoughts. Every look in the universe should inspire one about its Supreme Creator. Inspired by His presence everywhere speechless he/she says in the heart, *"We have no words to describe your Glory, no hearts to comprehend your praises. Indeed there is no god but you alone, You are the greatest ……………."*

Fikr (فکر) means the exploration and understanding of the creations of Allah. He loves those who explore deep in His works. The Qur'an has this to say on this, **"Worst of all Creatures are those who pass by signs of Allah, thoughtlessly."** Those who do not contemplate in the creations of Allah are condemned in the Holy Qur'an being rated lower than cattle's. It says **"They have hearts (mind) where with they understand not, eyes with which they see not, and ears where with they hear not. They are like cattle's – may be worse. They are heedless ignorant. 7(179)** Thus in the Qur'anic philosophy without Fikr one does not qualify even to be called a "Man".

Rasool-Allah (Peace be upon him) described 'Fikr' as the highest act of worship. He said, **"An hour spent in the contemplation of creations of Allah is better than the whole night spent standing in prayers".**

Indeed, we may see from the Holy Qur'an that one of essential character of a believer must be to reflect into the universe and everything in it. It says; *"Indeed the heavers and earth there are signs for the believers" 45(3), "And in your own creation, and the life Allah creates on earth, there are signs for the staunch believers" 45(4); And in the changeover of day and night, and (sources of) the livelihood which Allah sends down from the heavens and that with which earth becomes living after it is dead, and in the blowing of winds there are signs for the wise people 45(5),*

These and many more ayaat of the Holy Qur'an prove that faith is not complete with out serious contemplating in the Creatures of Allah. Thus scientific research and being abreast of knowledge of general science is must for every true believer.

Taskheer (تسخير) Refers to the conquest of nature, to put it to use for the good of mankind. Allah *Subhana-Hu* says in the Holy Qur'an, **"And He has subjected to you, as from Him, all that is in the heaven and on Earth. Behold in that are signs indeed for those who reflect into them thoughtfully" 45(13).** The same theme is repeatedly stressed in the Holy Qur'an in its various ayaat. The message is that everything in nature is made by Allah to serve you and His pleasure lies in that you put them to your service.

Thus, integrated together in his personality, a true Muslim represents a mystic's love for Allah, a scientist's insight for the creations of Allah, and an engineer's approach to mould the bounties of nature for the benefit of mankind.

Early Muslims were greatly inspired by these teachings of the Holy Qur'an; consequently, in less than hundred years they developed a civilization which was hungry for knowledge. With their qualities of "Zikr, Fikr and Taskheer" they served as the benevolent super power on earth for more than seven hundred years, till they lost this spirit of Islam. Then Europe took over from them but limited to the spirit of Fikr and Taskheer only. Even then they have reached where they are, Alas! They missed the spirit of Zikr and consequently have missed the development in the spiritual domain.

84
SELF ANALYSIS

Where I do stand in my Islam? This requires regular self analysis. In the following is the self-assessment questionnaire based upon the selections from the Holy Qur'an by brother Lt Col (R) Sheikh Abdul-Rauf[43].

If your answer is "yes", then evaluate your own rating positively out of the maxim allocated marks against each point.

If answer to any question is "No", then give yourself negative marks accordingly.

Negative answer to any of the first four questions renders one ineligible for the test.
Now go ahead with your self evaluation.

Below 2000	**Poor rating**
2000 – 3000	**Average rating**
3000 – 4000	**Good rating**
4000 – 5000	**Very good rating**
5000 – 6000	**Excellent**

---

[43] Sheikh Abdul Rauf, "The VISION – selection form the Holy Qur'an" page (326 – 336) Allem Publications 133-C Westridge-I Rawalpindi – Pakistan.

S. No	Question	Max. Marks Positive or Negative	Your assess-ment + / -
1.	You believe firmly and sincerely believe in Allah and that He has created mankind and jinns to worship Him.	200	
2.	You believe in the Qur'an as Revelation of Allah and try your best to understand it.	200	
3.	Fully believing in Kalima Tayyeba, you accept Prophet Muhammad (Peace be upon him) as the Last Prophet and try to follow him, and love him most.	200	
4.	You are conscious that the day is coming when you will be held answerable to the Almighty for your deeds and what the various parts of your body, - the tongue, the eyes, the ears, and the hands have been doing in the World.	200	
5.	You do not indulge in adultery, drinking and gambling.	200	
6.	You earn your livelihood by lawful means and advise others to do likewise.	200	

7.	You are regular in your Prayers and Fasting and you make sure that members of your household also observe them regularly.	200	
8.	When you can afford to do so, you offer sacrifice, give Tithes, pay Zakat (Mandatory Alms) and plan to perform Hajj (pilgrimage).	200	
9.	Believing in and endeavoring for martyrdom to be highly meritorious, you yearn for fighting in the way of Allah (jehad).	200	
10.	Considering usury as unlawful, you do not get involved into it.	100	
11.	Wherever possible, you enjoin good and forbid evil.	100	
12.	Neither do you deceive nor do you let others deceive you.	100	
13.	You treat your parents with respect and your children with affection and you give all of them share in your wealth accordingly.	100	
14.	You believe that all men are equal and you treat them as such.	100	
15.	You live peaceably with your neighbours and are not niggardly in lending articles of ordinary use to others.	100	

16.	You treat your relatives well; and try to arrange board and lodging for the orphan, the prisoner, the wayfarer, the poor, the needy and the indigent, as far as possible.	100	
17.	You are convinced that successful life can be led without falsehood, therefore one should always speak the truth.	100	
18.	You keep your promises and try to remain punctual.	100	
19.	You do not say things which you do not practice yourself.	100	
20.	You avoid suspecting people's motives, prying in their affairs and backbiting.	100	
21.	You never betray any trust.	100	
22.	You decide every matter justly even if it may adversely affect you.	100	
23.	You bear true witness and do not advocate the cause of cheats and criminals.	100	
24.	You take due care in matters of measurements and weight, etc.	100	
25.	You are honest and straightforward in your dealings.	100	

26.	Before making or accepting a recommendation, you make sure that it will not hurt the rights of anybody.	100	
27.	You are always affectionate and patient with your wife.	100	
28.	You try to 'remember' Allah's Holy Name while engaged in worldly preoccupations so that He always remains in your heart.	100	
29.	You invoke Praises and Salutations on the Holy Prophet regularly and frequently by reciting 'Salat-o-Salam' on him.	100	
30.	Instead of speculating about the nature of Almighty Allah, you ponder over His Attributes, and try to mould yourself accordingly.	100	
31.	You are very particular about the cleanliness of your dress and person.	100	
32.	You make due arrangement for the payment of your wife's dower in accordance with the marriage contract.	50	
33.	You enjoin on your children to earn their living by lawful means only.	50	
34.	You guard your modesty as a special gift from Allah.	50	

35.	As a woman When going outdoors you always use an outer covering around you to cover your beauty and adornments.	50	
36.	If is happy you are with Allah.	50	
37.	You know that compared to eternal life, your life in this world is like a drop in the ocean.	50	
38.	You start everything "in the Name of Allah, Most Gracious, Most Merciful" Whom you trust always for whatever you do.	50	
39.	You believe that you will get reward in proportion to your effort.	50	
40.	You are straightforward in speech.	50	
41.	You realize that amassing gold and silver will entail painful chastisement.	50	
42.	You are gentle in the use of power.	50	
43.	You neither niggardly nor extravagant.	50	
44.	You do not make Un-believers your friends.	50	
45.	You ask for permission and salute the inmates before entering other people's houses.	50	

46.	You eschew lewdness, indecency and slander.	50	
47.	You eat only lawful food.	50	
48.	You are not jealous of other people's superiority or prosperity.	50	
49.	In pursuit of earning a living, you eschew inordinate love of wealth.	50	
50.	As a seller, you do not dispose of defective goods without informing the buyer of their shortcoming.	50	
51.	You choose for others whatever you like for yourself.	50	
52.	Your avoid passing on anything based on hearsay and rumour without properly investigating it.	50	
53.	You are not jealous of others' superiority.	50	
54.	You admit as much right of your wife on you as you claim on her.	50	
55.	You arrange for the upbringing and education on your children in the best possible manner and make sure that their Islamic teachings are not neglected.	50	

56.	You conduct yourself in a manner that your spouse considers you to be the best companion or at-least a good man.	50	
57.	As an eligible female you avoid meeting a member of the opposite sex in privacy, believing that Satan is present between the two of you at such moments.	50	
58.	You believe that Allah has made man incharge of woman, to support and protect her, supply all her needs and run the household properly.	50	
59.	You admit as much right of your spouse on you as you claim on him.	50	
60.	You are always affectionate and obedient to your spouse.	50	
61.	You ignore and overlook your spouse mistakes and shortcomings.	50	
62.	You regard your spouse likes and desires like your own.	50	
63.	You limit your household expenditure to your husband's lawful income.	50	

64.	You worship Allah as though you are seeing Him in front of you and if that is not possible then at least you are aware that He is watching you.	50	
65.	You are always offering thanks to Allah for His blessings on you and asking for His Forgiveness.	50	
66.	You listen to the Qur'an with rapt attention while it is recited and you touch the Holy Book in a state of purity only.	50	
67.	You are constantly aware that Allah is watching you thoughts and deeds.	50	
68.	You try to remember death as much as possible.	50	
69.	You are firm believer in the fact; Allah has enabled you to choose between the paths of good and evil.	50	
70.	During the course of a problem, you look upon the tranquility caused in your heart as a 'noble' deed; and consider wavering and doubt as an 'evil' deed.	50	
71.	You discard what is doubtful and adopt such a thing which is free from doubt.	50	

72.	You are aware that if there is a gain it is from Allah, but for loss it is due to your own misdeeds.	50	
73.	You do not allow Devil (Satan) to place fear of poverty as a hurdle in the way of Charity.	50	
74.	You give Charity for Allah's pleasure and give the best in His way.	50	
75.	You do not show off while spending.	50	
76.	You are aware that Heaven lies under the mother's feet, and treat your parents kindly.	50	
77.	You subordinate your emotions to your intellect.	50	
78.	You give due importance to "Intention" and guard its purity.	50	
79.	You prefer the educated to the un-educated and try honestly to acquire knowledge.	50	
80.	You do not accept anything without ascertaining the truth.	50	
81.	You try to forgive people, especially while you are in anger.	50	
82.	You do not speak ill of others except when you have been wronged.	50	

83.	You say nothing of which you have no knowledge.	50	
84.	You are not haughty in your behaviour and are moderate in your dealings with others.	50	
85.	You are temperate in wealth and contented in poverty.	50	
86.	You are patient in misery.	50	
87.	You eat when you are hungry, and while there is still some appetite, you stop eating.	50	
88.	On doing good you feel pleasure; but on doing evil you are repentant.	50	
89.	While eating out of lawful foods or wearing permitted garments you are neither extravagant nor vain.	50	
90.	You are grateful to Allah when prosperous, and turn to Him for help when in need or trouble.	50	
91.	You answer harsh words with politeness.	50	
92.	You treat people with kindness.	50	
93.	You do not put a worker on a job without fixing his remuneration. And you pay wages to him before his perspiration dries up unless mutually agreed to otherwise.	50	

94.	You do not exceed limits while avenging oppression.	50	
95.	As an eligible marriageable male or female after your glance has fallen on a strange opposite set you do not give her a second look, believing that it would be deliberate and not counted as innocent.	50	
96.	As an eligible marriageable male you always try to avoid looking at a female's attractions.	50	
97.	You avoid meeting a member of the opposite sex in privacy, believing that Satan is present between the two of you at such moments.	50	
98.	You ignore and overlook your wife's mistakes and shortcomings.	50	
99.	In case of disagreement with your spouse you seek guidance from the Exalted Qur'an.	50	
100.	Your first glance has fallen on an eligible marriageable man or youth by chance, you do not give him a second look, believing that it would be deliberate and not counted as innocent.	50	
101.	You treat you step-children, if any, like your own children.	50	

102.	Seeing you is always a source of pleasure for your spouse.	50	
	Total	**7500**	

85
A MOMENT TO PAUSE AND PRAY

Unfortunately, a majority of the present day Muslims have become a cause of disgrace for the great ideals of Islam highlighted in this paper. Whereas the Deen of Islam is the quintessence of peace, progress and prosperity for mankind, many of its followers represent a living picture to the contrary. The reason why Muslims have earned disgrace and humiliation of the world is for their neglecting the teachings of the Holy Qur'an. The modern West has ascended the heights of technological development by adopting the grand legacy of Islamic civilization. Only if the Westerners adopted the spiritual heritage of Islam as well, they could claim to be the true believers in the present day. Sadly currently Islam is clouded by the ignorance of its followers, and the prejudice of its foes. But for the sake of peace, prosperity and happiness of the whole world, today more than ever before, there is an acute need to discover the true spirit of Islam. So let us pray to Allah and strive earnestly for the realization of our prayers.

O, Allah! O, Rabb of the universe, the Most Loving, the Most Kind and the Most Merciful: In the name of your last Messenger, Muhammad (Peace be upon him), we humbly pray;

Guide us on the right path of Islam, the religion of all your prophets, the path of those on whom you have showered your blessings. And give us courage to change what is undesirable; and strength to get over our failures.

Forgive us our shortcomings; save us from doubt; and keep us away from the path of those who have gone astray and earned your wrath.

Increase us in wisdom and knowledge; and show us the reality of things as they are, and bestow upon us the clear understanding of Your Revelation;

Fill our hearts with Your love, grant us understanding of Your creations and enable us to put them to use for the purpose you have made them for.

Make us beneficial for others, as it has been told by your messenger, the best among us is the one most beneficial to Your Creations.

Bestow us with a helping hand; a sharing nature and caring altitude. Your Prophet (Peace be upon him) had said, "The upper hand is better than the lower one"; Please Allah! Grant us that upper hand; with the means to support others.

Give us the courage to over ride our self interests, and strength to sacrifice for others what we desire for ourselves. Give us a contended heart.

Grant us the good of this world and the good of the world hereafter; and save us from the fire of greed, jealousy and enmity amongst ourselves and make life easy for us.

Please Allah! Whatever little good we may do, multiply it with your Grace. At our turns grant us a welcome death, and take us to Your special Jannat, among Your special servants; pleased with You, and you are pleased with them.

Ameen, O, Sustainer of the Worlds, Ameen! We submit to You, and to You alone.

Dear Readers,

Propagation of Islam is an obligatory duty (فرض) of every Muslim. Allah says in the Holy Qur'an, sura Al-Raad, ayat 40 (فانما عليك البلاغ و علينا الحساب) **"So upon you is to propagate and upon Us is the Reckoning".**

An easy way to discharge this duty is by the distribution of effective literature on Islam. The Holy Qur'an Research Foundation (Trust) offers to share this responsibility with you by providing its highly informative, effective and impressive publications at the much discounted rates. You can also order us to distribute them on your behalf. Please write us with your suggestions in the discharge of this duty.

TAHRIK-E-NOOR
60-C, Nazim-ud-Din Road, F-8/4, Islamabad.
Tel #: 051-2260001, 2282058
E-mail: sbm@darulhikmat.com,
Website: www.darulhikmat.com

www.ingramcontent.com/pod-product-compliance
Lightning Source LLC
Chambersburg PA
CBHW041624220426
43663CB00001B/4